Dedication

To my son,
who turned my life from black and white to Technicolor.

To my husband,
who healed all the broken parts of me.

I love you both.

Table of Contents

Introduction..5

Chapter 1: Origin Story..8

Chapter 2: Awakening..24

Chapter 3: Are You My Mother?..........................40

Chapter 4: New York...52

Chapter 5: Looking For Lloyd Dobler..................87

Chapter 6: Starbucks Saves Me...........................100

Chapter 7: Intuition & The Escape......................109

Chapter 8: The Narrow Room.............................121

Chapter 9: The Dead Speak.................................125

Chapter 10: Gifts & Curses..................................142

Chapter 11: The Ritual...154

Chapter 12: The Bridge..160

Chapter 13: The Pirate Witch Store............ 172

Chapter 14: The Seer..181

Introduction

I'm going to be honest—I've done everything I could to avoid writing this book. I've tried many times before, but always abandoned pages for TV, video games, or just the thought that, *"Hey, I talk to the dead... that's weird and hard enough."*

I've avoided writing this book because it's painful. I hate the past. As someone obsessed with the future, looking back almost feels like going against my nature.

I'm a psychic, right? I had to look up the spelling of that word—*psychic*—because I've hardly used it in years. That's another reason I avoided this. I call myself an intuitive and a medium, and those titles fit, but I recently came across a term: *futurist.* And I fell in love.

That's me. I love progress. I love what's next. I can see possible futures—the different path options we have—and I can predict beyond time and space. So why in the hell would I want to dive into the past?

I decided to write this book for one reason, and it's this: if my story can inspire you to keep going, to keep asking questions, to live true to yourself—whatever that may be. To know you're not alone. That the world is full of people in pain, lost, and hopeful for a better future. That the dead do not die. And even if you're sitting in your room, crying day after day, waiting for the light—I hope this can be that flicker.

I'm not going to tell you to keep dreaming or say, *"Dreams do come true."* I won't tell you, *"If I could do it all over again, I wouldn't change a thing."* Nope. I'll never say, *"It was meant to be."*

What I will say is: we choose our paths. Every choice we make creates a domino effect. One decision falls into the next and begins shaping different possible outcomes.

In my life, I've made lots—and lots—of decisions I wish I hadn't. And some I'm glad I did. But all of it was hard. And all of it was wonderful.

No one can promise you rainbows after the rain, but I can promise you this: you will grow.

This book is my story of that growth. And hopefully, if I can inspire you to take the next step, if I can offer any spark or even comfort in knowing we do not die—if I can be a part of your beautiful, painful path—then that's what pulled me away from playing *The Last of Us 2* to write this for you.

It's not popular to say as a human, but I love people. I love all the stories. I love knowing that so many of us are out there, just living, trying to find the door to our path.

That's why we're here, in case you're wondering. That's what I've come to understand.

Also—I don't have all the answers. If I did, I wouldn't be here. I'd be flying somewhere else.

I don't even have half the answers. Or a quarter. So if you came here for *all* the answers, you might be disappointed.

But through my work, I've heard over and over again from those who walk in other realms: *"Adela, you're only seeing a tiny corner of a larger puzzle."*

Still, I can share what I've come to understand. And I hope you take it from there.

What I've learned so far is this: life keeps moving—whether you're in this realm or the next. So remember this:

Follow yourself. Follow no one. Listen to your inner voice.

And if you learn nothing else from this book, I hope it gives you a break. A moment to laugh, reflect, or even just something to ponder between rounds of your favorite video game.

Chapter One
Origin Story

      The beginning of my life starts out like the plot of a Disney movie. And, like most of those movies, it begins with the death of a parent. My story is no different.

My mother, Ruthie, was a gentle, creative soul—kind, loving, quirky, and completely devoted to her children. She dreamed of being an actress, did some small-time theater, and loved anything creative. She was a free thinker.

She came from a home with a controlling, overbearing father—but one who was still well-loved and admired by the family. She grew up in a time when women had limited choices: get married to escape the house, or, if they were fortunate, go to college. Even then, they weren't expected to actually *use* their education. It was more of a status symbol, proof of good breeding and upbringing.

My mother did both. She went to university and married the first decent man she could find. My grandfather made sure his daughters married men who would always make money. He gave her husband a job and taught him how to run a business.

My grandfather was heavily connected to the Mob. He was never *in* it, officially—but he helped secure the financing they needed. It was never fully proven, just understood in our family, the stories passed around without much explanation. This didn't really change how anyone looked at him, except maybe his own children.

It wasn't easy having a father who would disappear at a moment's notice, only to return with a lot of money and no explanation. My grandmother never talked about the past, and everything I know came from other family members—stories with plenty of missing pieces. His nickname was Mickey, and his last name was Cohen. No, he wasn't *that* Mickey Cohen, but no one ever explained why that was his nickname.

My mother was the middle child. She had two sisters—my Aunt Sheila and my Aunt Miriam—and the three of them couldn't have been more different.

Aunt Miriam was drawn to glamour and glitz. She had a classic hourglass figure, like an old-school pinup girl. She wore tight sweaters that accentuated her large chest, and pants that hugged every curve. She had a heavy New York accent, a nervous laugh, and that's about all I remember of her.

She worked on the sets of major sitcoms as an on-set teacher. Back then, kids working in TV had to be educated on set between scenes. I remember she worked on the show *Silver Spoons*, and I was obsessed with Ricky Schroder. I begged her to let me meet him. She promised she would—and then canceled last minute. She said, "I won't treat him like a star. It makes him uncomfortable." That night, I yanked his picture off my wall and declared, "If I can't meet him, then forget it." I decided I'd rather crush on boys at school—at least I had a chance to talk to them.

Aunt Miriam never learned to drive. She only took cabs around Los Angeles, which was wild back in the eighties. No one did that. It was expensive and inconvenient—but she didn't care. She also got married at the Waldorf Astoria, which I always thought was a little extravagant. The photos from that wedding, tucked in my grandmother's album, looked unreal to me. A fairy tale. I think she divorced that guy, remarried, and had two kids.

One of her daughters passed away from pneumonia before I was born. Her son—he was my only cousin—and I loved him dearly. He was kind and gentle, always patient with me. He was smart, too, but had a lot of fears and quirks. Some people might have found him a little odd, but to me, he was just... him.

The youngest daughter, Sheila, was very smart. She used to claim she was a genius, quoting an IQ of 180. I don't know if that was true, but she sure said it often. She went to an Ivy League college—Cornell. Every time I think of it, I think of the show *The Office*, how Andy constantly name-drops Cornell and everyone acts like it's no big deal. Best show ever made. But back in the days when Sheila went, it *was* a big deal—and for a girl to go to an Ivy League school in the 1950s? That was serious bragging rights.

She went on to graduate school and earned a master's degree in history. She had her sights set on becoming a lawyer. She was an activist—outspoken against racism and injustice—and marched in the Civil Rights Movement. Sheila wasn't afraid to speak her mind. She had a natural leadership quality. People listened to her.

She also married outside of her race, which—being of Jewish descent—caused a ripple in the family. Her parents expected her to marry a nice Jewish man, preferably with a good job. Instead, in graduate school, she met a Jamaican man. They married and had two children at a time when interracial marriage was still deeply frowned upon.

Their marriage wasn't easy. He was highly intelligent and had a bright future ahead of him, but he treated her poorly. He had a drinking problem. A gambling problem. Eventually, she left him. Years later, I heard he went on to become a professor in psychology. He *did* have a future after all—but the damage had been done. I don't think Sheila ever fully healed from that relationship.

Now, she was a single mom raising two multiracial children in an era where people would say hateful things right to her face. She once told me about taking her kids to a restaurant where the waitress treated them horribly. Sheila left her a penny for a tip—on purpose—and then watched from the corner of the room just to see the waitress's face when she found it. She said the look on her face satisfied her. Back then, leaving a penny was a clear insult. These days, people would just assume you forgot a cent—or they'd film it for TikTok.

Even after her divorce, Sheila's activism didn't stop. She met my Uncle David at one of her civil rights meetings. He was a Black man from Detroit and had grown up Seventh-day Adventist—a religion that forbids meat, alcohol, and smoking. Sheila eventually gave up smoking and drinking for him… and maybe for herself.

She really liked him, but while they were dating he got deathly ill. His kidneys started to fail, and one day he was lying in bed at home, dying. The only person he could think to call was Sheila. He had never told her about his kidney disease. I guess he was afraid it would scare her off.

She rushed him to the ER, and after running tests, the doctor came out of the room and told her to go home. That he wasn't going to make it. She always told that story with a look that said she knew what they were really implying: *"What are you doing here with this Black man? He's not your husband. Go home."*

They gave him emergency treatment to try to clean the toxins out of his blood, but he was in severe kidney failure. His skin was pale ash. The poison his kidneys couldn't filter was seeping through his pores. That's what happens when your kidneys fail. The toxins build up in your bloodstream, and your body tries to push them out in any way it can.

They told her, *"We'll treat him. We can clean his kidneys. But it's not a cure, and he may not make it through the night. So go home. It's not your problem."*

If you knew Sheila, you'd know—telling her what to do never ended well for you. She told them, "No. I'm not going anywhere."

She wasn't the type to walk away from difficult things. One of the things she used to say often was, *"Life is difficult. Full of problems, but there is always a solution."*

He lived through the night.

At some point, she overheard doctors talking about a treatment called dialysis. At the time, it was still experimental. There was only one machine. She approached them and asked if it could be used on my uncle. She persuaded them to consider him. That's what she was good at—getting people to listen. Getting people to do things they hadn't planned on doing.

They told her he would have to petition for his life. There were other patients waiting, and only one machine available in all of Los Angeles. It was controversial, but this was the system they had.

I never really thought about it until now—the odds of her being there with him, in that exact moment in time. I don't believe in the idea that everything happens for a reason. I believe in decisions. It's the decisions we make that create the outcomes.

My aunt's decision to ignore the doctors and stay at the hospital... her decision to date him, even though she could've chosen an easier path, like her parents wanted... all of that led to her being right there, in that exact moment in time. And that moment changed my uncle's life.

It wasn't "meant to be." It was someone making decisions. And those decisions created a different outcome.

My aunt gathered all her civil rights activist friends and had them write letters to the hospital. She wasn't just going to hope—she took action. Meanwhile, the hospital staff conducted an interview with my uncle. They didn't tell him what it was for. He had no idea that his life was on the line. They wanted his answers to be authentic, unrehearsed.

They also took a few other things into consideration. He was young—late twenties, I believe—and he didn't drink or smoke. He had been a vegetarian his entire life, a lifestyle shaped by his upbringing in the Adventist church. His kidney failure wasn't the result of diabetes or substance abuse. It was simply due to kidney disease.

This was still an experiment. And for it to work, they needed a patient who could go the distance—who was mentally and physically able to handle the treatment, and who, from their perspective, was *worth* the effort. That's the cold truth of how experimental medicine often worked back then.

They chose him.

And the other patients didn't make it.

That weighed heavily on him. I know this because he went on to earn his PhD—managing to complete his studies from home—and wrote his entire thesis about the experience. I have a copy of it. I've read it cover to cover several times.

In it, he describes everything he went through. One part always stuck with me—his description of death. He called it *"a narrow room."* That phrase became the title of my first book.

He said the thing that pushed him to fight for his life during treatment was thinking about death in that way. I know that space he was talking about. It's a place I've seen in visions—an in-between, a liminal space between this world and the next. You don't fully die in the narrow room. But if you go beyond it… you've crossed over. You're home.

I guess he knew that too because, he didn't want to go there again.

I once asked him if he had a near-death experience. He said he did—but he wouldn't talk about it. He said, *"Maybe one day I'll write about it."* He never got the chance.

So here I am.

I believe the *narrow room* was a part of his experience. He went through hell and back. At one point he suffered temporary blindness. In those early days, they hadn't yet figured out that the dialysis tubing—the one that pulled blood out, filtered it through a man-made device, and then returned it—needed clamps. Without them, air bubbles could travel to the brain.

One day, that happened to him. The result was temporary amnesia, blindness, and paralysis.

But he survived, and that was just the beginning of what he endured.

At that time, they only had one machine, tucked away in a supply closet. They would wheel him in there alone, without a nurse, and tell him he had to stay awake in case anything went wrong. The treatment lasted twelve hours.

His dream had always been to become a doctor. And in a way, he did. He became Dr. Fulton, earning his doctorate in sociology. He also became a part of medical history. Because of his participation in that controversial treatment, many lives were later saved.

Sometimes I wonder how many racist people out there owe their lives to my uncle's sacrifice.

Years later, I had the chance to meet the man who created the petition system my uncle had to go through—Dr. Belding Scribner, the inventor of the Scribner shunt. Today, we call them ports. They're still used in dialysis and chemotherapy. He told me my uncle had been part of an elite group—only a handful of patients in the world at that time had survived as long as he did.

I asked Dr. Scribner, *"Do you think his spirit had anything to do with it? His positive attitude? His will to live—not just his body?"*
Dr. Scribner looked at me and said, *"Absolutely, yes."*

It felt good to have a world-renowned scientist confirm what I had always known: we are more than ones and zeros. My uncle's will, and the positive way he lived, had everything to do with his survival.

Eventually, my Uncle David and Aunt Sheila tied the knot. He could barely walk down the aisle—he was so weak—but they did it. My aunt wore a pink dress. My uncle wore his black Ray-Ban sunglasses. They were married now.

It took a while, but my grandparents came to love him. Really love him. And who wouldn't? He was a kind man. A good man. He believed in humanity.

My mother, Ruthie, was a romantic. She loved love. I often heard her described as whimsical but convicted. She lived a very free-spirited life. She valued art, creativity, and freedom. And the truth is—I don't know a lot about her. Sadly.

Someone once told me that if you had asked her, "Should I be a politician or an artist?" she would have absolutely said, *Be an artist.*

She had three children: my brother Harry, and my sisters Laurie and Cathy. I've changed some names—some I haven't.

She was a very loving mother. She treated her children like equal human beings. She cared what they thought and let them be themselves. She didn't believe in the idea that children should be seen and not heard. She slept on the couch so they could have the bedroom. She didn't care about material things or what people thought of her. She lived her life freely—and for herself.

She wore clothes that were too small for her voluptuous figure and didn't care if her stomach wasn't flat. She didn't have matching dishes or a picture-perfect home. She was described to me as a free spirit. She never held onto jobs for long, but when she did work, it was doing something she enjoyed. She was always taken care of by my grandfather. He made sure of that.

She divorced her first husband—an accountant, a very practical and reasonable man. It made sense on paper, but they were complete opposites. Eventually, she remarried. This time to a musician. I think she was looking for someone more like her—a fellow free spirit—but that didn't work out either, for many reasons.

She was now a single mom, twice divorced, with three children. Then in 1969, she met my father at a community center. He taught art. She taught acting. He was married. She didn't care. He was ten years younger. She didn't care. And at age 44, she found out she was pregnant—with me.

Everyone told her this was a mistake. Everyone told her not to have the baby. She was too old, they said. It could be dangerous. Let's be honest—people still feel that way today. She was a single mother, now pregnant with her fourth child, and the father was a married man. Again—she didn't care.

She saw me as a love child. She knew my father would never be involved, but she went through with the pregnancy anyway. When it came time to deliver, she chose my Uncle David to be in the delivery room with her. He was her calming force. A kind man. She chose him over her mother or her sisters. Choices set our futures. They carve the path. And her choice was my Uncle David.

He agreed without hesitation.

He told me the story many times—how he ran up and down the hospital stairs, updating the family, announcing every stage of the delivery. He told me that after I was born, she was so happy—and he was happy for her. He said he held me and wished I were his. He told me he loved me immediately and that my mother was brave and wonderful. He told me how honored he was that she chose him. And I believed him. I soaked up those stories every time.

She gave birth to me on August 19, 1970. I was a long, skinny, healthy baby girl. Everyone said she was radiant—truly happy.

After giving birth, she experienced heavy bleeding. The doctors encouraged her to have a hysterectomy. She refused. They managed to stop the bleeding with medication to help clot her blood and sent her home.

She was happy. She saw my birth as a fresh start. A new chapter.

I've been told that before I was born, she was unhappy. I never really knew why. Maybe it was empty nest syndrome. My sister Laurie was twenty when I was born, my brother Harry was twenty-one, and my sister Catherine was fourteen. I was never really told what was wrong, but it makes me feel loved knowing that she wanted me so badly—that she went against all odds and advice not to have me.

And I don't say this from a pro-life perspective. I say this from the deep longing of someone who knows very little about her mother. I never had much connection to her. So this—this story—is one of the few things that makes me feel close to her.

She brought me home. For ten days, she was my mother.

On August 30th, she was getting me dressed for a friend who was coming by to meet me. The hard part about retelling stories from before I was born is that I've heard them in so many different versions, from so many different people. But this part—this one—has always stayed consistent.

That day, she had been complaining of a headache and dizziness. After she laid me down in my crib, she walked out of the room... and collapsed to the floor outside my door.

She died right there.

My sister Catherine, only fourteen years old, was there with her. She saw it happen. She had to call the family and tell them. I can't imagine what she went through. And although we aren't close, my compassion and empathy for her never wavers. How could it?

My mother died of a pulmonary aneurysm.

But even that part of the story varies. Some say it was caused by my birth. That's why I've always had a hard time writing this part. It's painful. I've carried the guilt of her death for most of my life.

There's no light way to say this. No gentle way to wrap it.

She died. It was a blood clot. And it happened ten days after I was born.

Was it because of me? Or did she already have a blood clot?

I don't have a clear answer. I do know that blood clots are common after surgeries or deliveries like hers—especially when there's massive bleeding, clotting medications, and a refusal to undergo a hysterectomy. I believe those decisions had a lot to do with her death.

It's taken me a lifetime to be at peace with that. To not hate myself for it.

My intuition tells me it *was* related to the delivery and how her bleeding was handled. But I'm at peace with it now. I didn't make that decision. So I won't carry guilt or pain for others anymore.

After my mother died, I went to live with her sister—my Aunt Sheila—and her husband, my Uncle David. Both Catherine and I went to live with them.

There was a lot of debate over who I should go with. My brother Harry wanted to take me, but my aunt thought he was too young and too newly married. Aunt Sheila had been close to my mother, and they had made a pact—to take each other's children if anything ever happened. She was honoring her sister's wishes.

I was only ten days old. And even though I was a newborn, I believe that trauma left a mark on me—one I wasn't conscious of. My early childhood memories are sparse. Just blips and fragments.

Catherine stayed with us for a few years but left when she was nineteen and I was around five. Life with our aunt was much different for her. Aunt Sheila tried, but she lived a structured, academic, religious life—with lots of rules. I've heard both sides. My sister felt controlled and stifled. My cousins say their mom tried to help her.

Catherine was only fourteen when our mother died—of course she was traumatized. She should have had help. Maybe she did, but I was never privy to it. What I do know is that she didn't feel safe or comfortable. And when she finally left, it hurt my aunt deeply. She took it as a betrayal. And when you crossed my aunt, you paid for it.

After that, I wasn't allowed much contact with my sister. That's how she was. But my sister didn't try either. I lived in that house until I was eighteen and I never heard from her once. I understand it wasn't easy dealing with my aunt—but it affected me deeply.

I didn't see her again until I was in my early twenties. And I was the one who reached out.

So I don't know much about her—just the stories.

Once I moved in with my aunt, I was raised with her children, my cousins, but we were raised like siblings. I called my aunt "Mom," and my uncle "Dad." I always had a bond with him.

I guess he was right—he said he wished I was his daughter. And now, I was.

Did he predict that? I don't think so. But there's a part of me that wants to believe it.

I told you my story was like a Disney movie. Are you starting to see it?

From this point forward, I'll refer to my aunt and uncle as "Mom" and "Dad." But when I talk about my real mother—Ruthie—I'll call her that. My mother. She didn't give me up. She died. She deserves that title.

Still, I never felt like I fit into that family unit. And it wasn't just because of the multicultural upbringing. If *that* had been the only issue, it would've been easier to understand. My father was Mexican—so I was multiracial. But that wasn't the problem.

I just hated my childhood.

I looked at that time in my life as something I got through—not something I enjoyed. Maybe that's why I hate the past. I'm not a nostalgic person. I have very few pleasant memories.

But my dad was different. He was a kind, loving man, and I felt a connection to him. I don't really believe in the idea of "soul mates" in the traditional sense. I believe in *grow mates*—people we meet to evolve through. And I believe we have many types of soul connections—our friends, our pets... and for some of us, even our parents.

He was my *soul father*. I truly believe I knew him before I came here. That I chose him because I would need what he had to teach me.

I believe we pick our parents before we're born. We only get the CliffsNotes version of our life, and we're told the potential qualities our parents might bring to us. But we're also told they have free will. They can choose to grow—or not. Some do. Many don't.

I believe my dad did.

And I believe he was one of my soul mates.

Looking back, I think I read his soul. I saw beauty, compassion, kindness. I used to look into his eyes when I was little and tell him I could see his happiness. I told him he must be an alien—because he cheated death. He had no kidneys. After a failed transplant, he even had wires holding his organs together.

I told him he couldn't be human. He had superhuman powers.

He wasn't perfect, but I understood him. He came from a harsh childhood filled with neglect and abuse. But somehow, he came through it with a big heart—never angry, never jaded.

Every morning, he would raise one arm into the air and say, *"Oh God."* I asked him once why he said that.

He smiled and said, *"Because I'm alive."*

He was genuinely grateful for each day. Even the ones that followed dialysis treatments. He pushed forward. He never let it take him down. And that... astonished me.

He was private about his feelings—his real ones. I think my mom was the only person who truly knew him on that level. He had a way of putting on rose-colored glasses, seeing the world the way he wanted to. But honestly? Couldn't we all use a pair of those sometimes?

I just wish he had taken them off long enough to see how my mom treated me.

He saw the abuse. The screaming. The hitting. The emotional and psychological torment.

And he didn't stop her.

I never understood why—until much later. I intuitively believe it was hard for him to see the bad in a woman who had saved his life. Who had loved him even knowing he could die at any moment. I think he felt indebted to her.

I spent most of my childhood counting down the days until I turned eighteen so I could LEAVE.

Unfortunately, no magical fairy godmother ever arrived. No owl came to my window to send me to a hidden school of magic.

But something *was* starting to happen. My intuitive sight was growing. My ability to see spirits was becoming stronger. Premonitions in my dreams were unfolding more often.

It would take years before I truly understood any of it.

But, I would.

Because I was going to be the one to rescue me.

I was going to become my *own* fairy godmother.

And I was going to find my own magic.

This is where that journey begins.

Chapter Two
Awakening

Sitting in church and hating every minute of it was a standard Saturday afternoon. While most kids were waking up to cereal and Saturday morning cartoons in the '80s, I was waking up early for Bible School, followed by an afternoon church service.

I grew up in the Seventh-day Adventist church. And although it's not *officially* considered one, I call it a cult. It's not one of those flashy, bells-and-whistles kinds of cults. No—its entire message was about being humble, low-key, and *not* flashy. Having money was seen as materialistic... unless, of course, you were giving it to the church.

I went to a Black church. And for those of you who know the difference—you'll get this reference. Our pastor preached until his handkerchief was soaked with sweat and the offering plate was full of money.

For those who *don't* know that experience, let me set the scene.

One of my best friends went to a white church. She wasn't white—she was Filipino—but her church was. They went to service around 11:00 a.m. She skipped Bible School. There was a soft, monotone hymnal—very vanilla. Then came the announcements. The preacher gave his sermon, wrapped up around 12:10, and everyone filed out to the lobby for cookies and punch. After church, her family would head to a restaurant—which, by strict SDA standards, was a big no-no. Spending money on the Sabbath? Absolutely not. Sabbath lasted from Friday night to Saturday night, and going out to eat was breaking it. At least, that's how I saw it. I usually had to go home and wasn't allowed to join them.

But let me tell you—her entire church experience clocked in at a tight 90 minutes.

My church? That was a whole different story.

We arrived at 8:00 a.m. for Bible School. That's where I learned one thing: *don't ask questions.* Just absorb what they told you. That went until 11:00. Did we go home after that? Maybe relax a bit, have a snack, change clothes? Absolutely not.

Next came the pre-church mingling. That usually lasted until 11:30 a.m. or 11:45 a.m. And trust me—we never started on time. While my friend was sipping her punch and brushing cookie crumbs off her dress, we were just getting started.

The ushers wore white gloves and black-and-white uniforms. The deacons would come out. Then the choir. We had a few slow, dragging hymns that, to this day transport me right back to those dry, dreary pews.

But when the choir stood up? When *anyone* sang?

That was the only bright spot.
The music.

It was transcendent. Imagine Patti LaBelle, Whitney Houston, or Adele singing—*that* was the level of talent we had. In my church, and in many Black churches, this is where the angelic, powerhouse voices first took flight. Church was the stage. Church was where legends were born.

My best friend's dad had actually been the pastor of that church when we were little. Their whole family could sing—the dad, the mom, every single one of her brothers—and *her* too. The music was the only part of the service where I felt something spiritual. So I held onto that part for as long as I could.

But then came the announcements. The testimonies.

Most of them went like this: *"I needed money, and God sent a check in the mail."*

I wouldn't have minded that—it's not all that different from how I speak about the universe today. Except... I knew these people's lives. I knew how they talked, how they dressed, how they lived. And none of it matched up with the stories they were telling.

They smiled in their fine clothes and hats, and judged, and punished others for their "sins." They preached love and care—and then abandoned single, young pregnant women. So the testimony hour? That was a farce to me.

Finally, around 12:30 p.m., the sermon would begin.

The preacher would scream about how women shouldn't look like whores, how we were trash and dirt without Jesus, and how He died for our pathetic selves. Real uplifting stuff.

I would've sold my soul for an iPhone—anything to escape. But this was the 1980s. All I had was my mind, or maybe the string on my skirt, or the distraction of other people's children—who I was often the designated babysitter for. And I *loved* that.

Children, to me, were what Jesus—or God—was really about. They had light. Children showed us what love looked like. Acceptance. Hope. And yet, they were often the most undervalued, mistreated, and overlooked people in that whole place.

I guess that view came from my mother, Ruthie. She saw children that way too.

Church just dragged on. Most of my friends were there, and a lot of them went to my SDA school. It was complete indoctrination.

I was around sixteen at this point, already teetering on the edge of, *"Why do I need to be here?"* On this particular Sabbath, it was just my older brother and me at church. My mom wasn't feeling well, so she stayed home, and my dad took her to see a doctor. My brother drove us. We were obedient—we still went to church even without our parents. At least we'd skipped Bible School and wouldn't be staying for potluck.

At some point during the service, my brother was called to the phone in the church lobby. It was our mom. Everyone in our church knew our family. We were that "church-famous" family—the ones everyone went to for gatherings, the ones with "the voices," the community icons. Everyone *knew* us.

I always hated that. Our lives were constantly on display. It never felt real. I didn't feel a connection to the people or the beliefs. There's no room for authentic relationships under a watchful eye.

My brother and I were alarmed. We were used to worrying about our father. We had a sort of PTSD when it came to phone calls—they could mean something had happened to him. He was always living on the edge of life and death. If the phone rang at an odd time, our immediate response was always, *"What's wrong?"*

(If you grew up in a Jewish home, you know—"What's wrong?" is basically another way of saying hello.)

But this time, it wasn't about him. I didn't know how I knew, but I knew. My gut said it was about *her*. And in the psychic world, we call that a "knowing."

My brother came back into the sanctuary with a look that said everything. "Let's go." he said.

He didn't talk much—at least not in a deep, one-on-one way. He was charming, popular, good-looking. The life of the party. Everyone loved him. Same as my dad. My mom used to say that about both of them—they were "the light." They pulled people in.

My brother was the only one born from both of them. He was called a miracle baby, because at the time, no one knew if dialysis would affect fertility. Turns out—it didn't. My dad was the experiment, and my brother became part of the data.

Jared was so much like his dad. Charismatic. Charming. Saw the world through rose-colored glasses. But our personal connection? It didn't run deep. I didn't really know him. He was only three years older than me, but in those days, three years might as well have been a decade. Kids were expected to grow up fast. And he did.

He drove in silence. But I could feel the fear in him.

We were only ten minutes from home.

And here's what I remember most: My mom sat us down and said she had gone to the doctor.

She went to the doctor because she hadn't been feeling well for a long time. A doctor finally took a good look at her. Up until then, most had dismissed her symptoms as stress.

She had bumps all over her face, and every doctor told her it was late-onset acne—just outbreaks. My mom never wore makeup, but she loved skincare. Lotions and creams were her thing. Over time, she became more and more tired. She wasn't much of an exerciser, and she was overweight. Food was her comfort. Some of the symptoms, at a glance, did reflect her lifestyle—her health habits and her workaholic ways.

She sat us down and told us she thought it was the flu. But the doctor she saw that day recognized her symptoms. The first red flag wasn't acne at all—it was tiny blood vessels bursting under the skin of her face. That's what those "bumps" really were.

Women's healthcare was lacking in 1987—and it's still lacking now.

They ran blood tests. Her white blood cell count was extremely high. The doctor told her to come back for a spinal tap, and that we had to go—right now.

The family was in complete shock. We were prepared for something like this to happen with my father, but not with her.

My sister told me, years later, that I stood up and said, *"I killed one mother, I won't kill another."* I don't know if that's true. I don't even know if she actually said that to me. But it *feels* true to who I was. I knew about my mother Ruthie. I had known the story my whole life. They never shielded me from it.

I knew how she died. And even though they tried to soften the truth—saying they weren't *sure* how the blood clot formed—I felt what wasn't being said. Deep down, I knew they believed my birth caused it. Or at least, they feared it did.

So yes—I cried. And yes, it felt like I was cursed. And yes, I can believe I said something like that. My birth always felt like it brought nothing but pain, sadness, and darkness.

I don't even remember when the other siblings got to the house. But we all piled into the car and went to the hospital.

On the way there, everyone was making jokes. It was a common defense mechanism in our family. It had always been how we coped—especially with my father's chronic illness. Hospitals were like a second home. We knew how to do this. We'd been doing it for years.

But no one ever expected *her* to be the one in danger. Except me.
I *knew*.

I had been dreaming about her dying young for years—at least once a month. I always brushed it off as psychological trauma from losing my mother Ruthie. But deep down, I knew. It wasn't just trauma. It was a premonition.

The last dream I had of her was when I was fifteen. We were on the Santa Monica Pier—her favorite place. She loved the beach just as much as she loved the forest. Nature was her church.

In the dream, we were walking together on the pier, like we had so many times before. Suddenly, a hole opened beneath her, and she fell through. I looked down and saw her lying there.

I thought, *Oh no, she's hurt. I'm going to jump in and get her.*

But then a booming voice behind me said, *"You can't go after her. She died. You can't go in that hole—it's too dangerous."*

I didn't see a face. Just felt the presence. I've felt that presence before. A tall, powerful being who's always been there in my dreams. Some kind of teacher. A protector.

Eventually, I came to recognize him as St. Michael.

Now, I'm not Catholic. I don't even believe in traditional angels. But that name came up again and again in my journey. And something in me just *knew*—it was him. Or them. Those beings don't have gender. No being in that realm does.

It would take years for me to fully understand who he was. But I know now—I was seeing a vision. A true premonition. I was being shown her transition into the other realm. And I was stopped from following.

That was the last time I had that dream.

I used to have them so often, my mom always knew. If I knocked on her door in the middle of the night, she wouldn't even ask. She'd just say, *"Did you have the dream again?"* I'd say yes, and she'd let me sleep on the couch beside her bed.

She never seemed alarmed by it. If a child told *me* they kept seeing me die, I'd be shaken. But I think she chalked it up to unresolved grief. Just psychological residue from my mother Ruthie's death.

But I know now: the future isn't set in stone.

We can change it if we pay attention. The signs, the messages, the "knowings"—they're all trying to help us. Intuition is a gift. And if my mom had believed me... if she had listened to all those dreams... if she believed I was a *seer*...

Would that have changed her path?

I believe so.

But I can't say for sure. Because that time has passed. And now we're here, in this moment. In what was once the future.

Premonitions are real. That's what I now know those dreams were. They weren't trauma responses. They were glimpses. Guidance. Warnings.

But who was going to listen to an eight-year-old? A ten-year-old? An eleven, twelve, thirteen-year-old girl?

This is why I say to you now:

Follow your intuition.
Teach your children to follow theirs.

So when we were all sitting there in the hospital lobby and the doctor came out and said my mom had leukemia—that they needed to admit her immediately and begin aggressive chemo—I knew.

I knew this was what all my dreams had been about.

She lived for a year and a half after that.

During that time, she went through harsh chemo—awful, punishing chemo that almost killed her. But she made it through the initial rounds. She went into remission for about six months. Then it came back.

By then, I was sixteen going on seventeen. In fact, she was admitted just a few weeks before my seventeenth birthday. We celebrated—if you could call it that—while she was in the hospital. My siblings took me to a sad little diner. They tried. They were in their twenties, still young themselves. I know now that they were doing their best.

But all I could think about was how my birth always seemed to be tangled up with death. That thought haunted me.

When she came out of remission, I was around eighteen. It was the summer before she died. I became her caregiver. I drove her to chemo, to the beach—wherever she needed to go. Somehow, I was the one assigned to care for her. And that was when my awakening truly began.

I left the church. I left the church school. And I started to see things from a completely different perspective.

I began to understand things I never had before.

I saw that while her physical body was dying, her spirit was still alive. That our spirit is what actually runs us—that's who we *are*.

I saw her spirit, even though my human side was still angry, still hurt, and hadn't forgiven her. Not for the abuse. Not for the control. Not for the psychological damage. All of it messed with my mind.

And now here she was—vulnerable, dying—and I couldn't really tell her how I felt.

She needed me. And I was confused. How was I supposed to care for someone who had hurt me so deeply?

I wanted to feel love from her. But I never really did. Still, in those final months, I started to see *her*—the real, human version of her. Not the mask. Not the persona. Just her spirit. Her pain. Her unhealed wounds.

And *that* became a huge part of my awakening.

One day, she broke down crying on my shoulder. This woman who had always seemed larger than life, strong, in control—suddenly became a scared child. A woman filled with PTSD and emotional wounds bigger than I could understand at that age. But I *saw* them.

I washed her mouth when it filled with sores from chemo. She cried and told me she was embarrassed. She apologized. I felt compassion.

I told her it was okay.

I tried to comfort her—tried to stay stoic—while dealing with a tidal wave of mixed emotions. My mom was dying, and I didn't know how to feel.

Part of me kept thinking, *Maybe it's not that bad. Maybe she'll survive.*

But my intuitive self knew better.

I remember cleaning her blistered mouth and thinking, *Suffering shouldn't be part of human existence.* Not mine. Not hers. Not anyone's.

I helped her bathe. And sometimes, I resented her. Not just for being sick—but because I knew she might leave this world before I got any answers. Before we could resolve any of the pain between us.

I wanted to ask her so many things:

Why did you treat me so badly?
Do you blame me for your sister's death?
What did my real father actually say the day he came to see me after my mother died?
Why did you push him out? Did you give him the choice to tell his wife—or was it leave or lose everything?
What's the real story?
Why did you never let me call Ruthie my mother?
Why did my siblings all leave and never come back? Why didn't they visit me? Why did no one stay—except Laurie?

I had so many questions. But she was dying. And in my mind, *that* trumped childhood trauma.

We *did* talk about death, though. She told me I was the only one she could talk to about it. She said she felt like she could be honest with me.

I asked her if she was scared to die. And at first, she said yes

That changed after she came out of remission.

She started to say, *"Yes. I can feel I'm dying."*
And then, *"No. I'm no longer afraid."*

She looked and acted like a completely different person. Calm. Peaceful. It was strange—almost like she was already letting go of this world, slowly. And while a part of me felt relief for her, another part—deeper, younger, more wounded—was angry. Hurt. Because I knew I'd have to carry all the unresolved pain on my own now.

I had one of those moments you only ever see in movies. Small. Subtle. But, life-changing.

It didn't come with music swelling or tears falling. It came with silence, and a sentence that changed everything. It realigned something in me—restructured my inner world. Shifted my path forever.

It happened one day as I was driving her to the beach. I never took the freeway—I only went surface streets. Always the long way. My mother had been a terrible, nervous driver her whole life. She had no sense of direction. I definitely took after her in that way. I always joke that I can guide people on their *spiritual* path—but not the *earthly* one.

She was brilliant in so many ways, but driving wasn't one of them. She was a true New Yorker—born and raised—and didn't even learn to drive until she moved to L.A. at around thirty and I don't think it ever really stuck.

So that summer, I drove her—again and again—from the Valley to the beach. And I always avoided the freeways. I inherited that fear from her.

She was also the worst passenger. She'd grab your arm mid-drive, scream out loud, gasp dramatically—full panic. It was almost comical, but now I understand it for what it was: anxiety. Real, raw anxiety.

That day, she calmly told me, *"Take the 101."*

The 101 freeway.
The busiest, most chaotic freeway in Los Angeles.

I looked at her like she had two heads. "Um, no. Absolutely not."

If I was ever going to face that beast, it certainly wasn't going to be with my dying mother in the passenger seat—especially not the woman who once nearly caused an accident by screaming when someone turned left too fast.

She paused and looked at me.

And then she said, "Adela... I let fear stop me in life. Don't let it stop you. Now get on the freeway."

Something shifted in that moment.

She wasn't panicking. She wasn't controlling. She was calm. Stable. Peaceful.

And I trusted her.

For the first time, instead of fearing her, I leaned into her. And I merged onto the 101.

We drove in silence.

I *knew* that moment was special. I knew I'd remember it forever.
But I also knew, deep down, that she was going to die soon.

What I've come to learn through my work is this:
Dying is not just a process of the body.
It's a process of the *spirit*.
It needs time to let go. And that was what I was witnessing.

We arrived at the beach and from that day forward, I took the freeway to the ocean.

I began to see life differently.

I saw the *woman*, not the mother.
I saw the human. Not the role.

There's a quote that floats around the internet: *"Remember— it's your mom's first time being human too."*

I believe that.

Sometimes, it takes many years to reach the place where you see your parents not as gods, or monsters, but as *people*. That day was my moment. A bittersweet turning point.

But anytime I feel afraid, I still hear her voice in my head:

"Don't let fear stop you in life."
And I get back on that freeway.

Her death *was* my awakening.

Just like I believe my mother Ruthie's death opened something in me… so did this one.
Two sisters, bound by love and loss, shaped me.

One birthed me into the world.
The other raised me.

And I lost them both.

She died in early November. The day we spread her ashes at sea, I stood on the boat, watching her return to the ocean. And I heard her—clear as day—say:

"I leave you my strength."

I never told anyone that. But I *heard* her.
And I *felt* her.
And I knew—I was going to need that strength.

She had many fears and much pain, but she was the strongest, most badass woman I knew.

What hurt me was this: I saw that strength in her. I loved her for it but, I never felt that love come back to me.

Maybe it was our pain that kept us from reaching each other.
Maybe she did love me… and I just couldn't feel it.
Maybe she was angry that I never fully saw her as my mother—and maybe that hurt her.
Maybe we couldn't help each other.
Maybe our grief turned us against one another.

It's hard to read yourself.
And, even harder to make peace with a spirit.

But if anyone could try… it would be the budding medium.

I did love her.
I admired her.
I wanted to be close to her.
It just never happened.

Now, I was eighteen. I had lost two mothers.
And I loved them both, but I carried pain from both.

That day on the boat—like that day on the freeway—was magical.

I never shared it with anyone because I knew saying it out loud might take away the magic. It was for *me a*nd it was part of my awakening.

It didn't go unnoticed either, that the last time I had the dream of her dying… it was at the beach.

And now we were laying her ashes to rest in that same sea.

She left me her strength.

And I was going to need it—for the path that was opening up in front of me.

Chapter Three
Are You My Mother?

Love-seeking isn't always about romance.

When you're burned, damaged, and lost, you'll go looking for *any* kind of love. Some people chase the love of the masses—applause, praise, admiration. But, I always saw that kind of love as fleeting. One wrong move, one opinion the crowd doesn't like, and it vanishes. The love is taken away.

I didn't want that.

I wanted *respect*. I wanted someone to love *me*—the whole me. The parts I kept hidden. The ones that felt scary to show. But the truth was, I never *did* show those parts. I showed people my face. My body. My loyalty. My compassion. My anger. My pain.

I searched for *their* pain. Their bruises. Their lost souls. And when you go looking for that, it always finds you.

I felt very alone in the world.

I'd grown up with a mom who controlled every aspect of my life. When she died, I finally had a kind of freedom I had never known. But that freedom came with a cost. It also meant I was completely on my own—and I had no idea what I was doing.

I had stumbled into modeling—which I hated—but it led me to some interesting people and places.

At nineteen, I was working at a video store. I liked it. It was easy. I loved movies. The only part I hated was the dreaded back room. Yep—that one. The one with porn.

Ah, the golden days of the local video store—where you could rent *The Little Mermaid* in the front and *Busty Blondes 8* in the back, hidden behind a thin black curtain.

This was right when Blockbuster was starting to dominate the market by branding themselves as "family-friendly." That killed most of the competition. Sure, porn sells—but nobody wanted to shuffle through a beaded curtain while kids in the next aisle were grabbing Disney VHS tapes.

(And maybe—if I say "Disney" enough—they'll turn *this* into a movie.)

My manager at the video store was a total badass. She was pregnant, owned the place with her husband, and had her eyes on building an empire. I think they were planning to make it a chain here in L.A.

I was nineteen and I was impressed. She probably wasn't even thirty, and she seemed like she had her shit together. Meanwhile, I was driving a beat-up stick shift that ran on love, hope, and a prayer. It had no air conditioning, roll-up windows, and a clutch that stuck.

Still, I thought I was a badass just for knowing how to drive stick.

My job was to check videos in and out, shelve them—including the ones in the back room. A pretty big task for the square I was at the time.

But it was simple. I didn't complain and I loved movies. I was surviving.

It was around that time that I was at the beach with my sister when this couple kept staring at me. I was tall and skinny and deeply self-conscious. I saw myself as awkward, with no figure. But that day, for the first time, I wore a bikini.

The only thing I loved about myself physically was my hair. Long, brown, and really curly. When I was in junior high, I used to blow-dry it straight and spray the hell out of it with Aqua Net—classic '80s style. Teased in the middle, flat on the sides. Terrible.

Kids today try to recreate that "vintage" look. Why? It looked like a fried mess.

My mom used to beg me to wear it curly. I didn't believe it *could* curl. But one day, after she had died, I washed it and put product in, let it air dry—and I had full ringlets.

That became my signature look after that. (Though now I straighten it again—sorry, Mom.)

So there I was at the beach, standing awkwardly in a bikini, feeling totally exposed. I was still so innocent. I hadn't lost my virginity yet. I was a late bloomer. My religion had influenced that, for sure. And I'd spent most of my late teens caring for my sick mom so boys weren't really a priority.

I had this innate sense that losing myself in boys would only end badly. Same with drugs or alcohol. I knew I was vulnerable and if I gave in it might pull me into something I couldn't escape. So, I stayed away.

People would say, *"Wow, you're so mature. Like an old soul."*

But it wasn't maturity. It was intuition.

If I went down those roads, I could see where they ended. And it wasn't good.

So when this couple walked up to me and asked if I modeled, I was completely thrown.

"Me?" I laughed. "No. Not at all."

They told me I had an amazing "ethnic" look.
Insert eye roll here.

They asked how old I was. I said nineteen. They looked shocked.

"Wow, you look sixteen!"

Which, looking back, is extremely creepy. I've always looked younger than my age — I was used to that — but something about the way they reacted felt... off. Why did they seem to practically salivate?

They briefly explained they were a modeling agency and said if I was interested, I should let them know. The woman handed me her card. Back then, you had to look agencies up in an actual agency book, and I did — they were legit.

I ended up going to their office, where I immediately felt like a fish out of water. I was dressed like I was going to a job interview or church, and they didn't hesitate to point it out. The office itself was pretty bare — nothing flashy — but the woman had a raspy voice and this look in her eyes, like a tiger eyeing prey. I didn't fully understand that look until she kept talking.

She really saw potential — for both of us to make money. She kept saying, "I'm going to make you a star."

She had me at *making money.*

She said I needed a portfolio with headshots, which would cost money. That's normal—actors and models usually hire their own photographers. But when agencies start asking for fees up front? That's a red flag. Those places are scams.

She told me, "Go look at *Elle* magazine to learn poses."

I said, "Like... L?"
She looked confused. "You don't know the fashion magazine *Elle*?"

I shrugged. "Nope. My mom didn't let me look at fashion magazines. She didn't want me to grow up thinking I had to look like those girls."

She caught the irony. "Well, go look at them now," she snapped. Clearly, she couldn't care less why I hadn't.

She rattled off a list of magazines I needed to study for makeup, hair, and poses. When I finally bought a few, I had this weird moment of gratitude that my mom never let me near them. Same with Barbie dolls. She'd say, "Why play with dolls just to dress and undress them? What's the point?"

Which was *so* ironic—because she loved fashion. She took me shopping *all the time.*

She was full of contradictions.

She did encourage me to play with baby dolls, though. "Learning to be a mother is helpful," she'd say. And at the same time, she'd drill into my head, "A woman can be anything she wants."

I used to think, *Make up your mind, woman. Which is it?*

Turned out, I hated everything about modeling. *Hated* it. But I wanted money. What I thought would be *easy* money.

So if people wanted to pay me for how I looked? Fine.

A friend of mine loaned me $200 to do the photo shoot. It was in front of the Beverly Hills Hotel, with about six other girls. We were told to bring our "best" clothes. I showed up with skirts, nice tops, and jeans.

The photographer looked at my stuff and *scoffed*.
"Umm... maybe we can use this scarf," he said, like he was picking through a pile of rags.

He handed me a pair of jeans to wear and borrowed something from another girl to complete the outfit. Then he started complaining about all the *other* girls—to *me*.

"They're cute," he whispered, "but they're not real models."

I didn't even know what that meant. The girls looked like cheerleaders—pretty, short, not rail-thin. And in 1990, the look was rail-thin. Still, I felt bad for them. I thought he was awful.

Then he started calling me his "superstar."

He told me I was the only *real* model there.

Of course, the other girls instantly hated me. And who could blame them? He was pitting us against each other on purpose. Lining us up like cattle. Deep down, I didn't like him. But my insecure self... *liked* feeling special. Liked feeling seen.

Later, I found out that shooting a bunch of girls like that for their books wasn't normal. It was sketchy. He was clearly just there to make a buck. But he *was* a legit photographer—technically. He knew what he was doing.

Then he dropped the bomb:
"Uh, I don't have a permit to shoot here, so we gotta do this quick."

Wait—what?

I thought I was on some fancy shoot. He even had a hair and makeup person. But now I was realizing this was "guerrilla-style" shooting. Which meant… *illegal.*

I had no idea what a "headshot" really was. Growing up in L.A., I'd seen headshots in restaurants and dry cleaners—actors hoping to get discovered. But I'd never done one myself.

He told me, "Place your left hand up near your face and rest your fingers softly."

I raised my right hand instead.

"No, honey—your *other* left."

The way he said "honey," the way he implied I was stupid—my fuse was lit. I could feel the fire in my eyes.

This idiot photographer just *talked to me* like that?

I glared at him, switched hands, and said sharply, "I *know* my left from my right."

He saw the look in my eyes—and clicked the shutter.

"Perfect," he said.

That ended up being the best headshot I've ever taken. The agency loved it. I used it for *years*. People always commented on how intense my eyes looked.

"You look amazing in this—so fierce. So sexy."

Sexy?

No. I was *furious*.

That, right there, sums up what it's like to be a woman.

They saw sexy.
I saw pain.

I didn't like modeling. Not at all. But I had no college degree. No real skills. No help. I was alone. I was lost. And I *wanted* to feel loved. I wanted validation. So I went for it.

I needed gas money just to get to "go-sees"—the model version of auditions. I needed better clothes. I had to learn how to walk, how to pose, how to apply makeup.

My job at the video store was perfect for that. It kept me afloat.

And it was easy to get sent to go-sees. It wasn't hard to get an agent. I'd walk into some building in Hollywood or downtown, hand over my portfolio, and stand there while they flipped through it. They'd ask for my age, size me up, snap a Polaroid…

They always wanted to see you without makeup. Even then—without Photoshop—girls knew how to make themselves look thinner and taller just using angles. Most of them lied on their comp cards about height and weight. A comp card had a few pictures, your measurements, height, and weight—your "stats."

People were always surprised that mine actually matched what they saw in person.

The thing is, I never gave a shit about any of it.

The other girls looked desperate, like they *needed* this. I didn't. I wasn't there to become a star. I didn't care about magazines. Newspaper ads? Great. I heard they paid more anyway because you couldn't use them to build a career.

So what? I just wanted to get paid.

But over and over again, I heard: *"You're so ethnic. So different."*

That was code for: *You're not white. You don't have blonde hair or blue eyes.*

This was the '90s, and girls like me were told we were better suited for New York or Europe. In Los Angeles, it was mostly music videos or commercials—and I was "too ethnic" for commercials.

I once had an agent tell me, "If you had blonde hair and blue eyes with your bone structure, you'd book every day."

The modeling world was brutal. They didn't care about your feelings. But my feelings didn't get hurt—because I wasn't in it for validation. I was in it for *money*.

So I came up with a plan.

I needed to get to New York.

That's where the agencies were. That's where I belonged. I kept hearing it over and over.

And then, one day, a tall woman with long blonde hair and blue eyes walked into the video store and started talking to me. I told her I wanted to go to New York.

She came back with:
"I'm on a mission. I'm going to get you to New York."

She said those exact words: *"I'm on a mission."*

It hit me in the chest. That's something my mother *always* used to say when she helped people.

I was in this huge spiritual awakening, and I *swore* my mom was speaking through her.

So I said, "Wow. Okay."

I trusted her instantly.

I was lost. Looking for love. Looking for a mother figure.
I was spiritually wide open.

My favorite book as a kid had been *Are You My Mother?* by P.D. Eastman.

The story's about a little bird whose egg hatches while its mother is out getting food. The baby bird doesn't know what to do, so it leaves the nest and goes around asking everyone it meets:

"Are you my mother?"

A cow. A dog. A boat. A *forklift*. Every time: "Are you my mother?"
And every time: *No.*
Until finally, the forklift puts the baby bird back in the nest. And the mom returns—just in time—with a worm in her mouth.
The baby bird snuggles into her and says, *"I know you're my mother."*

I read that book over and over again as a child.

Maybe I had always been looking for my mother.

And when you're lost and broken, *vampires and predators will find you.*
They smell blood.

My heart and energy were wide open.
She used both to pull me in.

Next thing I know, I'm buying a plane ticket from the newspaper.
Back then, you could do that—buy other people's tickets from classifieds. They didn't even check ID.

Nancy found a one-way ticket to New York for $150 and bought it.

Her name was Nancy. I went to her house one night to pick up some clothes she was giving me for the cold weather. I sat in my car while she brought down bags from her apartment.

She stood there in the dark, and I swear she had a glow around her.
A gold light. Soft and warm.

She handed me the clothes and said, "You'll need warm things for New York."

I looked at her and asked, completely sincerely:
"Are you an angel?"

Poor young Adela. My heart was so open.
Are you my mother?

Even writing this now, I feel for that girl.

Nancy seemed to glow. She laughed and said, "No… but something like that."

And I believed her.
She saw my soul. She *wanted* to help me. She believed in me.

My family didn't. I felt misunderstood. But Nancy *got me*.
And even better—she *wanted* to help.

I took the clothes. I quit my job. I told my dad I was going to New York.

He pushed back, but not that hard.

I told him, "I'll make it."
He didn't really ask where I was staying.
I didn't really know.

Nancy had arranged something. A friend of hers. Some older man who worked in government. It felt like a magical movie where the fairy godmother finally shows up. I was Cinderella. And Nancy had arrived.

Of course, looking back, we all know better. But in that moment—I *believed*.

I had found someone who saw me.
Someone who would help me.

My dad drove me to the airport. I remember the sadness in his eyes. I felt his pain. The pain of losing his wife. The pain of not knowing what to say or do.

And my own pain—the pain of feeling utterly lost, and deciding:
I guess I'm truly on my own.

Deep down, I wished my father had stopped me.
I wished he'd said, *"Don't go. It's dangerous. I'll help you. What do you need? Who are you? And how can I help you be that person?"*

But instead, he just sat quiet—like he always did in those days.

He waved goodbye.

So, I left for New York.
Nineteen years old. No real plan. $300 in my pocket.
And a one-way ticket.

Chapter Four
New York

So here's the backstory:

      The first time I went to New York was in high school. We had a class trip there, and I fell in love with it immediately. Maybe that's what sparked the need to go back. That first trip was filled with sadness, and even though I knew it was a place I wanted to return to one day, I had no idea I'd be back so soon.

Before my mom died, I had switched schools. I went back to the Waldorf school I had attended in kindergarten and first grade. Waldorf is a private, non-religious school founded by Rudolf Steiner, who's very well known in the occult world—something I had *no* awareness of at the time.

Steiner's philosophy was that children are magical and that their magic should be protected. He saw how connected children were to the unseen world and believed in nurturing that connection. Waldorf encourages this kind of magic. I attended when I was little but had to leave because in Waldorf, you stay with the same teacher from grades one through eight. You switch classrooms every year—but not teachers.

The idea is to cultivate a long-term relationship with a teacher—fostering trust, safety, and emotional continuity. That's the upside. The downside? If you're assigned a teacher you don't like, you're stuck with them for eight years.

My mom didn't like my first-grade teacher, so she pulled me out and placed me in a Seventh-day Adventist school. It was an odd decision. I was a magical, sensitive, and intuitive child—out of the four of us, I was the one most connected to unseen things. She took me out of *Hogwarts*—and trust me, every friend I've brought to that school since has called it that.

Waldorf believed in teaching reading *later*. They emphasized storytelling over phonics. Teachers would create stories from scratch, draw them in beautiful colored chalk on blackboards, and we'd recreate them with beeswax crayons—because Steiner believed beeswax had magical properties. It was a whole experience: imaginative, visual, emotionally alive.

We would draw the stories before learning to read the words.

Because of this slow-burn approach, by second grade, I still didn't know how to read. That's when the new school suggested I be held back a grade. I remember my parents breaking the news—I cried so much. My best friend from church was also at this school, and I thought we'd be in the same grade. For a little kid, it was devastating.

The Adventist school was the complete opposite of Waldorf. There were strict rules, workbooks, Bible study, and discipline. We made nothing. Waldorf had us *make* our own books, hand-drawn and hand-written. Here, everything was printed worksheets and memorization. Religion was taught right alongside math and reading.

My first-grade teacher was kind. But it was downhill after that.

I remember my second-grade teacher pounding her fists on desks and screaming at us. She even *taped my mouth shut*. I kept thinking, *I left my magical school for this? This is what loving God looks like?*

It wasn't a Catholic school with rulers and nuns—but it wasn't far off.

My mom had originally pulled me from Waldorf because my first-grade teacher used to make us stand on desks with our arms and legs crossed if we got in trouble. She didn't like that. But this? SDA school was worse.

When I returned to Waldorf in high school, some of the students told me that same teacher my mom disliked had turned out to be amazing. That stung. Because I never wanted to leave that school in the first place.

Now I was in a rigid, religious environment instead of a magical one.
It made no sense.

Years later, I told my dad about the mouth-taping incident. He acted like he'd never heard of it. I found that hard to believe—I was *known* for not keeping secrets. I can't imagine I didn't tell them.

I learned *nothing* in that school. Their money didn't go to real education—it went into teaching the Bible. Why care about science when Jesus would rise and lift all the bodies to heaven? Why teach evolution when God created everything in seven days?

So I survived until eleventh grade. Midway through the year—with my sister's help—I finally left. I transferred back to Waldorf.

That's when I met kids who smoked, drank, and did drugs… but who also showed deep compassion about my mom's illness. The teachers knew my family and were understanding. It was a totally different world.

What confused me at the time was: *Why did my religious parents choose Waldorf at all?*

Later, my sister told me my mom had discovered the school early on. She loved how open and liberal it was. She liked the flexibility it offered, especially with our dad's illness and her unpredictable schedule. My mom hadn't always been so heavily involved in the church. She was raised Jewish, turned atheist, and then later joined the Adventist church—mostly for my dad.

So my older siblings, Aub and Tanya, weren't as indoctrinated as I was.

My brother Jared left Waldorf after graduating eighth grade.

Waldorf attracted a lot of well-known families—including Harrison Ford's kids.

My brother was best friends with Harrison Ford's son, Ben. We always called him *Mr. Ford*—the same way we'd address any parent. He wasn't famous yet, and even when he did become famous, it was just proper etiquette to refer to adults as Mr. or Mrs. So-and-so.

We knew about *Star Wars* before the world did.

I remember talking about it at school when I was in kindergarten—around 1976.
(Yeah, yeah—don't do the math. I'm still young.)

It was around the time they started shooting *A New Hope*. The details are a little foggy, but I *do* remember the excitement. My friends and I whispered about it—Ben's dad was going to be in a sci-fi movie called *Star Wars*. Back then, sci-fi wasn't taken seriously. Nobody could have predicted what it would become.

At our Waldorf school, there were about 17 kids in a class. It was close-knit—like a family. No one was treated differently, and I think that's part of why some celebrity parents sent their kids there. To give them something resembling a normal life.

They even hosted a fundraiser for the school—a private screening of *Star Wars* for all the families. That's how small they thought the movie would be.

My brother and I weren't allowed to attend.

Our family's Seventh-day Adventist beliefs had strict rules: **No movies.**

Can you imagine?
We had an exclusive *Star Wars* premiere… and our parents didn't let us go.

I'm pretty sure we were the only family that didn't attend.

Ben even gave out some early merch from the film—things with typos. Posters, t-shirts. He gave my brother this plastic-looking trophy that said **STR Wars**—the "A" was missing. It sat in his room for *years*. I'd ask him all the time, "When are you going to toss that thing?" And he'd say, *"Never."*

Years later, I met this guy who was a massive *Star Wars* fan. I told him about the trophy. He practically lost his mind. "Misspelled merch is worth a *ton*!" he said. "You *have* to call your brother. Like, right now."

I called him later that day.
My brother said, "Sadly, no. I don't have it anymore."

After our mom died, in the move from our house to a townhouse, my dad lost some things. They'd been in storage. That trophy was one of them.

I guess my psychic abilities didn't foresee how valuable that plastic thing would be.
The Force was not with me. (*Sorry, I had to.*)

Our school was also invited to *The Empire Strikes Back* premiere.
Again—we couldn't go.

If you're a *Star Wars* fan reading this, I'm sure it hurts as much to hear as it does for me to write.

Now, when I go to Disneyland and walk through Star Wars Land, I think how insane it is that *we were there at the beginning.*

Before Harrison Ford blew up, he personally built a small shop for our school to sell snacks, candles, books. It's still there.

One of the reasons my brother left Waldorf was because he couldn't attend those events. After missing the *A New Hope* and *The Empire Strikes Back* screenings, he was done.

The year after I returned to Waldorf—12th grade—my school planned a class trip to New York. We were in California, so a cross-country class trip felt incredibly elite.

It was.

The trip was meant for us to meet our Waldorf "sister school" in New York.

My mom wasn't working. She was very, very sick. Money wasn't flowing like usual. I wasn't planning to go—but someone, anonymously, paid for my trip.

My mom was dying. I didn't want to leave her.

But, I also wanted to see where she had grown up.

She was slipping away. It was becoming clear she'd need hospice soon.
But she was still coherent.

I asked her if she wanted me to go.
I told her I didn't want to leave her.
I was too afraid.

But she insisted.

I really can't recall my mom's exact words, but I remember her pushing me to go.
She never went back to New York after all those years.
So it felt like... I was doing this *for* her.

I decided to go.

Our class sponsor made sure I had an open return ticket—something you could buy back then. You could purchase a ticket that didn't lock in your return date, so you could leave when you needed to. It was one small reassurance in a time when nothing felt safe.

I went to New York—and I *fell in love*.

The city. The noise. The people. The smell of street pretzels and pizza. Everything reminded me of my mom, my grandparents. It *felt* like home.

She always talked about New York pizza—the kind you fold. The hot pretzels you could buy from a cart. The delis with the best cheesecake, bagels, and egg creams.

Every time we ate cheesecake in L.A., she'd say, "Doesn't taste like New York."

It was dirty. Grim. Raw. It was 1988 New York—not the sanitized version we know now and I loved every inch of it.

When our class arrived, our hosts gave us a crash course in survival.
"Don't make eye contact on the subway."
Got it.

We did all the tourist things—Central Park, the Statue of Liberty (we even climbed all the way up into the crown, which you can't do anymore). It felt like we were walking through another world.

Our sponsor, Mrs. B, told us she'd gotten us tickets to a brand-new Broadway musical.
She said, *"You'll thank me later. This one will go down as a classic."*

We all kind of rolled our eyes, like... okay, sure.

The musical?
Phantom of the Opera.
With the original cast.

The moment that chandelier crashed down and the music swelled, we were all leaning forward in our seats—spellbound. Hypnotized.

Mrs. B, if you're reading this somehow—thank you.

Thank you for knowing we'd look back on that night in awe. For giving us something legendary when everything in my life was falling apart.

I loved New York so much. I vowed I'd come back. Maybe even move there someday.

The trip was magical—but I was in a *very* dark place the entire time.

I didn't know if my mother would still be alive by the time I got home. There were no cell phones. Every time we went out for the day, I'd rush back just to call home.

Our sister Waldorf school hosted us, and I stayed with one of the teachers along with my best friend, Kia. Every night, I'd call a family member. I'd ask, *"How is she?"*

They'd always say the same thing: *"She's okay. Try to enjoy your time."*

Enjoy?
Really?
How?

In photos from that trip, I look so young—and so *sad*. I see the sorrow in my eyes, like a dark cloud trailing me. I carried the dread of what I *knew* was coming.

One night, I returned after a long day of touring. I was told immediately:
"Call home."

My heart pounded as it always did.
But, this time was different.

My family told me I needed to come back.
My mom was in a coma.
She didn't have much longer.

I broke down, sobbing.

The teacher whose home we were staying in didn't come out of her room to console me.
Later, I found out she had gotten into a fight with Mrs. B and was mad about her not spending time with her. She was *pouting* while I was falling apart.

Mrs. B told me later that she yelled at her.
"Go help her. Her mother is dying."
But she refused.

Looking back now? That's *insane*. A grown woman being petty while a teenager breaks down in her guest room.

Mrs. B came and picked me up herself—in a black town car.
I thought it was the fanciest thing in the world.

My best friend Kia wanted to fly home with me.
I told her no.
"Why ruin your trip? I'll be with my family. Stay and enjoy it."

I think that was pretty mature for an 18-year-old.
More mature than Mrs. B's best friend, for sure.

I remember the whole class watching me get into the car.
I barely knew them, so I wasn't emotional about *them*. But I could see it in their faces: *Glad it's not me.*

When I was 16, my best friend's mother died. I didn't know she had cancer. She'd never said a word. At the funeral, we walked up to the casket together, hand in hand. It was the first time I'd ever seen a dead body. In Jewish tradition, we bury quickly—no open caskets.

She squeezed my hand and cried.
Her family was Jamaican—very stoic with emotion.
I remember thinking how strong she was.

And I remember thinking, deep down: *This could be me.*

Now it *was* me.
And all those eyes were on me.

I kept my emotions in check, just like she had.
I don't remember boarding the plane. But I remember *being* on it.

I sat next to a couple who asked me the usual small talk questions.
"So where are you going? What's the plan?"

I lied.

I said I was going to visit family.
I didn't want to say, *"I'm flying across the country to see if my mother is dead or alive."*
I wasn't about to cry to strangers.

I kept getting up to run to the bathroom. At one point, I pulled the blanket over my head, laid my face on the tray table, and tried not to cry.

I laugh now thinking about it.
They probably thought I was either crazy or doing coke.

No one told me there was a phone on the plane.
I could've just… called home.
But, maybe it was better that way.

When I got off the plane, my sister Laurie was there to meet me.
I could tell from her face.

"She's still alive," she said.

We went straight to the hospital.

My mother was tied to the bed.
Skin and bones. A wisp of herself.

I found out later they'd restrained her because she kept screaming, getting up. The bleeding in her brain was causing erratic behavior. Her leukemia had thinned her blood so badly it had spread into her brain.

I sat beside her and held her hand.

The nurse stepped out while I talked to her…

About a year later, I found myself on a plane back to New York. I had $300 in my pocket and no plan.

I sat next to a stranger who looked at the name on my ticket and said it out loud.
He said, *"I'm the one who sold you that ticket."*

He started talking to me about life paths—how the universe has a way of guiding us. I had never had anyone speak to me like that before. He talked about energy, how important it is to let it guide you. That nothing is an accident.

I was like a sponge.
My heart and spirit were wide open. My soul was looking for answers—and here he was, delivering them. The whole flight, I soaked in every word.

By the time we landed, there was a bond. I trusted him.
But my intuition whispered to me, *Something feels off.*

I ignored it. It's hard to hear your intuition when you want so badly to believe.

He asked how I was getting to my destination. I told him I planned to take the bus.
He said it wasn't safe, not at that time of night.
He offered to drive me.

My mind said, *Are you insane?*
But my gut said, *You'll be okay.*

He rented a car. I felt taken care of. I was floating—high on hope, excitement, the energy of the city.

The whole drive, he spoke kindly about me and my path. He told me, *"This is just the beginning."*

I looked out the window, mesmerized by the lights of the city.
He saw my gifts. He understood me.
He believed in me—even though we'd just met.

His words circled in my head. My heart was wide open.

Are you my mother?

We arrived at the apartment Nancy had set up for me. It was huge. Beautiful.

We stepped onto the balcony, and I gazed out at the night sky.
He said, *"Look at the city. Look around. This whole world is yours."*

I stood there, taking in the lights, feeling like I was on top of the world.
I believed every word.

He left after that.
He never touched me. Never made any attempt.

I was convinced I had just experienced something magical—something spiritual.

I walked around the apartment in awe.
Two bedrooms. A huge living room. Giant glass windows glowing with city light.

How did I end up here?

Nancy had arranged it all. It was her friend's place—some kind of European diplomat.
I called her. She was excited and told me I had the apartment to myself for a week until he returned.

I toured the building.
On one floor, there was a private video store for residents.
Another floor had a salon and a sauna.
I had never seen anything like it.

I went to different modeling agencies and landed a meeting at Wilhelmina—one of the top agencies in New York.

It was freezing. I had all the wrong clothes. My feet froze in the snow. My jacket was too thin.

But, I didn't care.

I went ice skating at Rockefeller Center, my feet numb—but I felt more free than I ever had in my life.

Then I—

heard someone calling my name—or did I?
I did.

I looked up, and someone I knew from back home was at the top of Rockefeller Center, calling out to me. How was this happening? Someone from back home?

I took off my skates and ran up to her.

Looking back now, I believe the universe sent her to me. If I had told her everything that had happened—the plane ride, the man who drove me, the apartment I was staying in—I'm positive she would have seen the red flags. She would've picked up on all the signs of possible trafficking or grooming.

But instead, I smiled, acted like I was living my best life, and talked about how great everything was.

The universe sometimes screams at you… but most of the time, it whispers.

It had been a week, and the diplomat was back. I no longer had the apartment to myself. The magic spell didn't break—just cracked.

The first night he was there, I found him interesting. He seemed intelligent and refined, but nerdy in a way. He was tall and slim, with short, curly hair and large glasses. He wore a dress shirt and slacks—exactly what you'd expect a diplomat to wear.

There was a huge piano in his living room, and he played it for me. I knew he was trying to seduce me, but I felt more amused than anything. His intentions were obvious, and although that *should* have scared me, it didn't.

He was 36. And in some strange way, my intuition saw him as weak.
I knew I had the power.

I was young and beautiful—a model in New York. Him hitting on me didn't feel special at all.

He said, "You're so special," and showered me with compliments.
I laughed.
"I'm a 19-year-old model in New York. Of course you like me."

He looked surprised. I could tell he didn't expect that response. My intuition had come back online, but I was also curious. Where was this all leading?

He told me he was taking me out to dinner. I went to my room to get ready. He went to his. I could hear the phone ring and I heard him say Nancy's name.

I then overheard him say,
"Yes, yes… she's nice, she's beautiful… but I'm not going to marry her."

Ping.

My intuition was in full blast mode now.
Why were they having this conversation about me?
Why did it sound like I had been *ordered*?

My instincts were screaming, but my longing to stay in New York was creating static on the connection.

We went to dinner. It was fancy. Everyone there was older than me. There were other women and men—some of the women had accents. They didn't talk to me much. I had an odd feeling I was being sized up.

The diplomat asked me what I wanted to drink. I was confused—wasn't I underage? But he was European, and I figured maybe things were different. Still, my gut said something was off. I declined.

He looked disappointed, confused, and a little frustrated.

The food was excellent. The drinks kept flowing. He asked again if I wanted something to drink. Again, I said no.

By this point, my gut was on full alert. I knew I needed to keep my head clear. If I drank, the alcohol would go right through me. I'd only had a few glasses of wine in my life, always with my sister. Never anything strong. Something felt *very* off.

We left the restaurant, and one of the European women came with us. The others left.

We went to a club called The Limelight. It was a church that had been turned into a nightclub.

When we arrived, I didn't think they'd let me in. But they did. The doorman seemed to recognize him. We skipped the line. We were let in immediately.

I'd never been to anything like it.
It was dark, with multiple floors.
Some floors had *beds* on them.

It was gothic and intense—for me at least.

He and the woman were drunk. He was all over her.
I wanted to leave… but where would I go?

I was staying with him. He was paying for everything. I didn't know where we were. I didn't know how to get back.

I sensed what he was trying to do.
He wanted me to *join* them.

So I stayed far away. I kept moving. If they went to one side of the club, I went to the other. All my walls were up.

He kept asking if I wanted a drink.
I kept saying no.
He was getting frustrated.

"What's wrong?" he said. "Dance. Drink."

I told him, "Go be with her. I'm fine here."

He left me alone. And I stood there, fully clear on what was happening.

He thought I'd loosen up. Join them.
He was mistaken.

We finally left.
In the cab ride back, they were kissing and petting each other.

I felt sick.

We arrived back at the apartment.
I went straight to my room.

The woman was sitting on the couch. Her makeup was smeared, her hair a mess—she looked drunk and dirty to me. I asked, "Do you want something to sleep in?" I decided to be kind to her. I felt like she was lost, too… but it was too late for her in life. For some reason, I wanted her to know I didn't blame her for the night.

He came into my room, kissed me, and said goodnight.
I wanted to throw up.

I knew then—I needed to get out of there first thing in the morning.

I called one of my best friends, Rose, and told her, "Stay on the phone with me all night."
I told her *everything*. I said, "Let's run up this motherfucker's phone bill. He can afford it."

I told her I could hear them on the couch, and she told me to look.
I was too scared. But, I wanted to see.
If I'd been a full adult, maybe I would've known how to handle it—but I wasn't. And I didn't.

I told Rose to hold on. I went out to the bathroom, passed the couch, and I saw him—on top of her.
He froze when I came out.

I heard her whisper, "She saw us."
He whispered back, "She's fine."

I grabbed a robe from the bathroom and ran back.
I picked up the phone and told Rose what I saw.
She said, "Ew!" and we both laughed at the absurdity—but I was still scared.

I called Nancy that morning. She acted surprised, but my gut told me she wasn't.
I ignored it.

My intuition told me she knew this was the plan, but I just didn't fall for it.
She told me her roommate—Bill—was going to fly out to help me.
She said his *brother* had an apartment, and I could go there. That I'd be safe.

I was so touched by her "help" that I let any suspicion go.

I had to pack, but my suitcases were in *his* closet.
I tiptoed into his room and saw him sleeping in the bed—with her.

I don't know why I cared. I didn't love or even like this man. He disgusted me.

But I suppose I just didn't feel special anymore—just discarded.

I grabbed my suitcase, packed, and got dressed. I went to the front door—it was thick and heavy. I pulled on it, heart pounding. It wouldn't budge at first. I panicked.

Then it finally opened, and when I closed it, it slammed loudly.
Shit.

I ran to the elevator.

I heard the thick door open behind me.
The diplomat appeared—standing there in his underwear.

The elevator doors opened just in time. He ran up to me and said,
"What are you doing?"

I said, "I'm leaving. Seems obvious, doesn't it?"

He said, "But, I'm responsible for you!"

I looked him dead in the eyes and said, "Not anymore."

The elevator doors slammed shut.
I remember thinking, *This is like a scene out of a movie.*

I went down. The doorman saw me—saw how stressed I looked.
I asked him if he could get me a cab.
He said, "Of course."

He had a look like he'd seen this before.
I said, "I need to get out of here."
And he replied, something like, "I don't blame you."

At that point, I *knew* this was all a setup.
But I still hadn't fully pieced it together—Nancy planned it, the guy on the plane was part of it, and maybe even the name on the ticket was some other girl who wised up before her New York trip.

Looking back now, it's all *so* clear.

This is how girls get trafficked.
It's subtle. It's dressed up as glamorous.
But my intuition saved me.

I did stay with Nancy's roommate's brother—and Bill, the roommate, flew out to help me.
Bill never mistreated me. He was kind.

Eventually, I flew back to L.A.—broken, sick, and confused.

I called my brother Aubyn. I had an opportunity to stay in New York, with another agency—just as big as Wilhelmina, maybe even better.
I asked him, "Should I stay?"

He was the logical one. He said,
"I think you pushed it. Come home."

He paid for my flight and I went back to L.A.

For years, I wondered—if I had stayed, would my path have been easier? Would I have made money? Seen the world?

Part of me felt like I gave in to fear. But my intuition knew my brother was right.

I was now back in L.A.—wiser, but still very lost.
Spiritually, though, I was wide open.
And Nancy was waiting... oh-so-kindly... to take advantage of that.

Nancy had this apartment with her two kids.
She was the *first* person who really saw whatever this gift was that I had.
And she also knew how to use it—for her benefit.

I would show up at her house and she'd have my favorite candy.
"How did you know?" I'd ask.
She'd just smile and say, "I know a lot."

She seemed *magic*. A psychic. *Something*.

What people don't realize is that in the spiritual and magical world, there are many people waiting to take advantage.
It's a *huge* problem.

So many people exploit open-hearted, open-minded people.

I was wandering the streets of my life—and Nancy was happy to play savior.

She'd say strange things.
She'd act like my mother's spirit was talking to her.
She took me to see *Interview with the Vampire* and said she swore she could *be* a vampire.
Crazy things.

And honestly? I almost believed her.

She had this way of glowing.
Until one day—she didn't.

One day, I looked at her and it was like whatever "spell" she had cast just *dropped*.

I had been spending so much time with her.
She was only about ten years older than me—maybe more—but I saw her as a mother figure.

Are you my mother?

I never thought she cast a spell on me—more like she *manipulated* me.
I was a very innocent nineteen-year-old.

When I type *nineteen*, I realize just how young that really is.
But at the time—

I had lost two mothers, suffered through abuse, and had a spiritual awakening. I felt more like 29—but I wasn't. My spiritual heart was wide open.

I do believe Nancy had abilities, but she was most effective at taking advantage of a grieving, lost young girl.
That's not magic. That's just manipulation.

I was out in the world. No money. No help.

One night, I was driving home from Nancy's house—it was around 2:00 a.m.—and I got pulled over. As soon as I saw the flashing lights, I knew I was in trouble.

I hadn't paid my car registration. And back then, in L.A., you could actually get *arrested* for that.
I also had a few unpaid tickets, and I think one might've gone to warrant.

Still… for expired tags?

Two officers walked up to my window—a man and a woman. The female officer asked me to step out. She asked if the car was mine.
I said yes, heart beating out of my chest.

She asked if I knew I had unpaid tickets. I said I did.
She asked why I hadn't paid them. I told her, "My mom died. Life has been hard."
She didn't care. Not even a little.

She glared at me.

Then she asked if I had $2,500 on me.
Of course I didn't.

She smirked, and on went the handcuffs.
She seemed to enjoy having that kind of power over me.

Over *me*?

I had a plaid shirt on. Jeans. My hair was in a bun. I weighed 125 pounds soaking wet.
And she was enjoying this moment. For *expired tags*.

The fear that took over me was beyond anything I'd felt before.

They brought me to the police station and handcuffed me to a bench.
The male cop played "good cop." He whispered, "I don't know why she's insisting on arresting you. She's new on the job."

I believed him.
I even thought he felt bad for me.

She was bragging about me—like I was a big catch.
Now I just laugh. *Me?*

They let me call my dad.
He sounded tired. He said he didn't have the money to get me out.
He felt cold. Maybe he just didn't know what to do. Maybe his depression had paralyzed him.

I was crushed.
And I was scared.

I realized, *I really am on my own.*

As much as my mom hurt me in life, if I had called her from jail at two in the morning., she'd have been there in minutes.

This was the work she did—she ran a nonprofit for teens in trouble.
She even took mybrother and I to Juvenile Hall once. We pretended to be "troubled kids" for a video project. She

showed us the cells and said,
"You don't ever want to end up in a place like this."

She didn't believe in letting kids have a "night in jail" to teach them a lesson.
She said it would damage someone for life. *One night—anything could go wrong.*

I don't think my dad felt any differently. He just seemed… lost. He was used to her handling things like this.

While I sat on the bench, they handed me another ticket.
They said it was for the expired registration.

This is the system.
The less you have, the more they take.

I was learning life lessons fast.

They took me downtown to the *real* jail—and holy shit, was that terrifying.

But surprisingly, the women in there were kind to me.
They knew I didn't belong there.
They kept saying, "What are you doing here?"

One girl asked what my parents did.
I told her my mom had died, but my dad was a professor.

She said, "Wow. I wish I had a father like that."
I paused, realizing what she meant.

She just wished she had someone "normal."
Someone who took care of her.

It stopped me in my tracks.
I never looked at my life the same way again after that.

Most of the women in there were in for drugs, selling their bodies—and/or petty crimes.
Some *wanted* to be there, just to get off the streets.

I realized I had stepped into a whole world of hidden women.

I was innocent, but I wasn't naive.
I had street smarts—or maybe I just knew how to read the room.
I stayed quiet. Stayed small. Stayed inside my lane.

One girl asked if I'd ever even smoked weed.
I whispered, "No."

She *howled* with laughter and screamed it across the cell: "Did you hear that?! This girl's never even smoked weed!"

My heart stopped.

My attempt to stay invisible just blew up in my face.

But then, some of the older women—women who looked like they'd been in and out of jail for years—spoke up.

"Good for her," one said. "Maybe we wouldn't be here if we were like that."

The girl got quiet. Paused. And then said, "Yeah… you're right."

I also realized that if you act like a badass when you're really just a soft square girl, they won't respect you. But if you show who you truly are, they might. Those old timers in jail did. Or at least they saw me as no threat—and the other girl backed off.

I realized life was a series of decisions. And one always affects the other.
I also learned that what separates a rich addict from a poor

addict is just that—**money**.
I went to school with kids who were rich and did every drug under the sun, but they'd never wind up in a cell like that. Their status protected them.

Nancy got me out of jail.
I had been in there for two days—it felt like two years.

She told the judge my father was sick, a dialysis patient. She said she got the bail money from my sister. It wasn't even bail—it was just a processing fee.
And then, Nancy decided that she and her friend and I would take that money and go to Vegas.

I was still under her spell—but mostly, I was so grateful she got me out.
She was the only one who convinced the lawyer. So I saw her as my hero.

I saw my dad in the courtroom.
He looked broken. I was so angry that he let me stay in jail that long.
Later, I found out he was angry, too—angry that Nancy had used the fact that he was on dialysis to manipulate the judge into releasing me.

I thought, *Who the fuck cares? I got out!*
Why did he care so much? Was his pride more important than my safety?

My family thought I was in some cult-like situation.
They weren't wrong.

I was torn, but I went to Las Vegas with Nancy.
I was in too deep.

Only recently did I realize—and yes, I know how dumb this sounds—that she was definitely a sex trafficker.

Not the type who grabs girls off the street.
She was the type who lures them in with promises of money and power.

And I started to catch on.
I also had this sixth sense that kept whispering:
GET OUT. GET AWAY FROM HER.

But she made it all feel so *fun*.
So free.
Just run away. Live your life. It felt like freedom.

When we came back from Vegas, my sister was freaking out. At the time, I didn't see the problem. I saw it like a little break after a hellish experience. It felt like I was just floating—finally having someone take care of me.

Even if it was all delusional.

I had no idea Nancy never paid my sister back.

My sister later told me that when Nancy came to her house, she looked up and thought: *She's a witch.*
Little did she know—nor did I—Nancy was, in fact, involved in the occult.

Somehow, my sister picked up on her energy.

Things got odder and odder.
At one point, I realized Nancy was trying to lure me in *sexually*.
Not overtly—subtly. Like a game.

And I was aware.
Somewhere in me, I *knew* what she was doing.

But I kept pushing that knowing down, convincing myself, *She's not crazy. She's just different.*

That thinking would get me into trouble with many people in my life.

Still, the feeling kept growing. Something wasn't right.

In the witch world, there's something called **glamouring**—where someone can cast an illusion, making others see what they want them to see.

Her glamour started to break.
And as I began to pull away, suddenly—she broke her foot.
Now she *needed* my help.

That made me feel obligated.
So I stayed. I babysat. I helped her.

One night, she hobbled out on a date and left me with her two boys.
They looked innocent—cute, even.

But as soon as she left, the one with chubby cheeks turned to me and said:
"My mom's not here. I'm not innocent. You can't tell me what to do."

It was insane. I swear, it was like *Chucky*.

I was thrown. What the hell was going on?

Nancy often slept with men to get money out of them.
I started to see it clearly.
All while she was living with a man she had somehow convinced to pay for everything.

Then one day, she took me to a man's house.
He was clearly wealthy. The house was huge.

As I descended the stairs, I saw her sitting with him at the dining room table.

And I swear—I heard her in my head say: *"We can get his money."*

And in my mind, I responded: *"No."*

She laughed out loud.
Then turned to him and said, "She's very gifted. She can hear my thoughts—and I can hear hers."

I didn't know what was happening.
Was I losing it?

But deep down, I *knew* it was real.
And I also knew—no one would believe me.

That's the problem with paranormal and magical experiences.
When *you* see it, *you* know it's real.
But the world?
It shuts it down. It dismisses it.

So you're alone in it.

And there are people who prey on that aloneness.
They see your gift—and they exploit it.
Just like any other kind of talent or vulnerability.

I started to catch on, and one night when the guy she lived with had enough. It was his apartment, and he was kicking her out. She started freaking out and acting crazy. I had invited my friend over earlier to hang out. My friend was lost too, but definitely more grounded than me. She was also more sexually experienced and told me later she felt Nancy was absolutely trying to seduce me. She said the way we laid together was like a couple. I had no sexual feelings toward her, so I didn't see it. I said, "No, she's like a mom or an aunt." Today, this would be called grooming, but back then, I thought I was grown and knew my way around the world. I was in so much pain, I'd have joined the circus if it meant feeling less sad, less alone, less scared. I guess that's like Pinocchio. I was a lost girl looking for a place to fit in, looking for love.

She told me to scare the guy she lived with. She wanted us to taunt him. Then she even said, "I have a gun. Go get it." To this day, I think she was lying, but even so, I stopped her. I said, "I'm not doing anything like that." She implied she wanted to hold it for protection. He was a big guy, but like a sheepdog—all bark, no bite. He just kept saying sorry and looking at us. I didn't get their dynamic until much later. I realized she manipulated him, teased him with sex, used him. She was a con. But a con who definitely knew magic and had gifts of her own.

Not long after, I really started to wake up from my slumber of escapism and began to challenge her. One day, after she broke her foot, I was helping her wash dishes. She slammed the faucet down and said, "Be quiet!" Her face turned ugly, evil, disgusting. I guess the glamour broke. She had gone from love-bombing me—feeding me, dressing me, praising me—to expecting me to serve her. Yes, broken people are easy to manipulate, but she was right: I had a gift. And I felt like I was repeating my childhood. Someone was trying to control me and shrink me. It felt like she was trying to break me. That would be a recurring theme in my life. But if someone is trying to break you, it's because you have something they want. Never forget that.

I also had this odd feeling she was doing some kind of magic to keep me there. What kind, I had no idea. I had never met a witch or known witchcraft. I went from a sheltered world and slammed right into the real one. I started to leave her house more and more. Then suddenly, her lung collapsed and she was in the hospital. I didn't live with her, but I was at her house all the time.

Now I know this sounds insane, but I swore she was either faking it or somehow made it happen. Looking back, I believe it was fake. I went to the hospital, and her mother—whom I had never met—was there. She was wearing a necklace. I lifted it, looked at it, and she said, "Yes, that's what you think it is. Don't be afraid." I think it was a pentagram.

That was the moment. I knew something was way off, and I had to get far, far away.

I'm not trying to feed into conspiracy or cast a bad light on witches. This wasn't about magic. This was about manipulation. Real witches don't feel evil, but people who take advantage of lost girls? They do.

I stuck around just long enough for her to get out of the hospital. I never got the full story on her or her background. She once claimed her father lived in an expensive hotel. I believed her. One time we drove by it and she said, "My dad lives there." That was it. No explanation. Just more confusion—on purpose.

Years later, I met a real witch—a pretty powerful one. I told him about her and asked, "What was that?" He said, "It's like a test. You meet those who try to pull you to the dark side." He told me I passed.

I laughed and said, "This is some Star Wars shit."

One day, I drove her to look at stoves. I don't even remember why. I had already made plans. I called a friend and said, "Pick me up at this time, at this address. Keep the car running."

Somehow, Nancy knew I was done.

While we were eating, she looked at me and said, "Guess you won't be my wife or help me get money from men." She said it like a joke.

I didn't know or care why she said it. All I knew was I had to get the fuck out. It felt more like, "Guess you're not the one. Guess I can't groom you."

I thought, *Damn right.*

I said, "Nope. Guess not."

We went to her house. I grabbed my stuff. My friend pulled up. And just before I could leave, she looked at me with her star-blue eyes and said, "I won't be seeing you again, right?"

She knew.

Even though I had lied and told her I was just going home for a minute, she knew.

I said, "No."

I ran to the car, jumped in, and screamed, "GO! GO! AND DON'T LOOK BACK!"

I literally felt like Nancy had some kind of power that could stop us.

We drove off, and shortly after, I moved into my sister's house in Northern California.

I was so freaked out that I left L.A. entirely.

While I was there, I had a dream; Nancy was flying, calling my name.

Now I know what you're thinking. Sounds like *The Craft*, right?

Nancy was the evil witch. The girl with the natural gift. Mother died after birth. The blue eyes. Yeah, I thought that too. Nancy is her real name- by the way.

But all this happened *before* that movie came out. 1989–1990. *The Craft* wasn't released until May of 1996. I did tell my story many times. I moved back to L.A. two years later, four years before the movie dropped.

I'm not saying that was my story. But growing up in L..A, I've seen how stories float. Writers listen. Things get repurposed. I'm not saying someone stole my life, but when I saw that movie, it was *way* too close to home.

At the time, I wasn't worried someone stole my story. I was paranoid that Nancy told someone hers.

I even heard her calling my name in my room. I told my sister, and she said, "If you keep saying this, I'm going to have to admit you."

So I stopped. That's why people don't talk about paranormal experiences. That's why I created my podcast, *The House Medium*—so people know they're not alone.

Shameless plug: Listen wherever you get your podcasts.

Here's what ended up happening. My awareness of my gifts happened. I had a dream. I saw her flying at me, calling my name, telling me to leave my sister's house. And then, in my dream, a tall man appeared. He said, "You are the light. She's the dark. You have the power. Take this dagger and shrink her. Use the dagger."

So I did.

In the dream, she got smaller and smaller.

I yelled, "You're the dark! I'm the light! GO!"

I stopped dreaming of her.

Later, my friend told me Nancy had called to ask where I was and when I was coming back. My friend lied and told her she didn't know.

So yes. I believe it wasn't just a dream.

Chapter Five
Looking For Lloyd Dobler

I was 21 years old, now living in Northern California. I initially went up for a visit with a friend, drawn there by a boy—that didn't work out. I had dated him right after graduating high school for only a few weeks. He was older than me—22—and I'd never really dated before. I fell pretty hard. He was my first at everything—well, not everything. I still had my V card.

I followed my intuition a lot in my life, not realizing that's what I was doing. Somehow, I knew he was the wrong person to give that to. I wanted to be in love, to feel safe. And although he looked like a model and came from a well-to-do Seventh Day Adventist family, he didn't feel genuine.

He tracked me down after seeing me once at my brother's house. My brother was a college professor and had invited his students over for a movie—some case study for his psych class. I can't recall what movie it was because I was too busy staring at him. Later, I found out he spotted me there and asked my brother for my number. He wasn't even a student— he was a friend of one of the students. When my brother called and asked if I wanted him to give out my number, I didn't hesitate. Of course! My brother Aub was always respectful, great with boundaries. He could be analytical, but I appreciated how protective he was.

I lit up from the inside, that feeling you get when you're young and full of hope and light. I felt special somehow. I had just seen the movie *Say Anything* and thought, this is the kind of love I want—someone supportive, a little edgy, but kind. He wasn't anything like John Cusack's character. Maybe that's why I didn't fully trust him.

I told him about the movie. I said, "We have to watch this!" I was so excited. After it ended, I turned to him and said, "Wasn't that great?" He paused and replied, "Well, if I was in high school, maybe. It's a little immature." I wanted to scream, *"Fuck off, you're only three years older!"* I should've known right then—it would never work. He was no Lloyd Dobler.

Still, he was my first kiss and when he invited me to his father's yacht for an overnight, I declined. We spent three whirlwind weeks together, and at the end, when he asked me again to come spend the night alone with him I had a flash—a vision of myself devastated. So, I said no.

He had a twin sister, and we became friends. At first, maybe it was because of him, but soon I really liked her. We grew close. I'm sure it was weird for him. It's not like we had been together long—we weren't engaged, hadn't even slept together. We just dated for a short while and his sister still sends me holiday cards.

So, when she asked if I wanted to drive up to Northern California with her, I jumped at the chance to see my sister. I hadn't seen her brother in a while, but he decided at the last minute to come along. Interesting, I thought. He lived there, sure—but why did he want to spend six hours alone in a car with me? I definitely assumed it was about me.

I spontaneously decided to stay in Northern California and moved in with my sister Tanya. She'd been asking me for a while. After the hell I went through with Nancy, I jumped at the chance. I had no life back home—my father was depressed all the time and wasn't helping me.

Within a week, I enrolled in school and got my first job working in a preschool. I was excited. I'd loved kids my whole life and thought maybe I'd make a career of it. I didn't really want to go to college, but I figured it would make my family happy.

I come from an extremely academic family. My father, as I've mentioned, was a college professor and so was my brother Aubyn. Junior college wasn't exactly up to their standards, but it was better than nothing.

I told the boy I'd moved, and of course his response was, "I hope not for me." I scoffed. "Of course not! It's for me—for my sister, to help her with my nephew. I was going to anyway." I lied. It *was* for him. But it was also for me. I was lost. Clearly chasing love. Chasing something. Maybe love. Maybe answers. I didn't know. I didn't understand why I kept cheapening myself like so many of us do just to get a little attention.

College was okay, but it had its weirdness. I was trying to find myself. I'd always been around my family growing up. I came from a multiracial family, and most people knew my background. But now I was in the real world, knowing no one. It felt so divided. Black students didn't seem to want to be my friend. On campus, it was divided in the courtyard—people sat by ethnicity. It was odd, and I didn't know where I fit in.

One day I sat in the area where all the Black students gathered, and no one talked to me. I wasn't used to this sort of divide. There did seem to be a lot of racial tension. It was Northern California, but not San Francisco—a different vibe in the suburbs.

My whole life I was sort of immersed in Black culture, and now white people were accepting me based on how I looked. I loved R&B and soul music. They would talk to me about rock music or use lingo that wasn't my way of talking. I was trying to figure out who I was in this world, alone.

I joined the theater class. I had always wanted to try acting and it turns out I was actually really good at it. I loved it. I think because I'm so intuitive and know how to be empathetic and absorb energy, I naturally did well. The teacher, on the other hand, was an asshole. You know how some artists decide to teach, and then they're resentful about it? That was him.

The first scene we were assigned was a monologue. I chose one from the play *Nuts*, which was also made into a movie starring Barbra Streisand. The story is about a woman who was a sex worker and is accused of killing her client. Her lawyer is trying to prove she's not crazy—that she had real reasons for doing what she did. There's an iconic monologue where she speaks to her mother about the abuse she suffered from her father. In the movie, they show a scene where her father slips a dollar bill under the bathroom door while she's a teenager in the bath, crying, and he's knocking, begging to be let in. Then it cuts back to her on the stand. The first lines should have won Streisand an Oscar.

The monologue starts: "When I was a little girl, I used to say to her, I love you to the moon and back again. And she used to say to me, I love you to the sun and down again and around the stars and back again. Do you remember, Mama?" Streisand pauses. Those first lines tell you everything. She's asking her mother, Why? Why didn't you protect me? You knew he was in that bathroom with me. You saw. I trusted you. And you said you loved me.

I understood her pain. I didn't have the same experience—no one molested me—but I understood the pain of feeling unprotected and abandoned. I chose that monologue. I had an old hospital gown that had belonged to my father. Not sure why I had it, but I wore it to school to copy the scene from the movie. I went up on stage, nervous but ready. My heart was pounding, but once I started, something else took over. I pictured my mother in the audience. The words came from my soul and flowed out. I could see her face. I think I was talking to both of my mothers—a sense of abandonment. I wasn't sure. I knew they had died, but emotions aren't logical. I didn't care what anyone thought. I just lost myself in the moment and tried to heal something inside me.

Afterward, silence. Then loud applause. We had a sub that day, which was disappointing. I wished my teacher had seen my performance. What I did that day wasn't just acting. Not all the way.

The next time, we had to do a partner scene. I scanned the room and saw a quiet girl. I got a read on her. I could feel she would be great for a comedy scene. The class was full of loud, dramatic theater kids. Most people would have picked them. But we turned out to be an amazing pair. I loved her quirky ways. She took me to a cool coffee shop and gave me what I thought was chocolate candy. I popped those so fast. We talked, laughed, bonded. I really, really liked her. Turned out they were chocolate-covered espresso beans. No wonder she was so ON. We found a dark comedy about two girls who kidnap a pizza delivery guy and debate whether to have their way with him. I played the straight one, she played the quirky loud one. We practiced a lot and put so much effort into it. I loved her free spirit and how she didn't care what people thought.

Before our big scene, the teacher invited us to a play he was directing. I went, hoping it would earn me points. It was that play where they spend most of the time on a raft—I think it was Mark Twain? Can't remember. What I do remember: four people in white t-shirts pulling the raft. Lights full blast. No attempt to make us believe they were on a river. I think I left early.

The next day, he asked who went to the play. Hands went up. All the theater kids praised it. I raised mine and said, "Um, I did." He asked what I thought. I said, "Well, the people pulling the raft were very distracting." He glared. "Well, what should I have done? This isn't Broadway. I don't have a stage to pull a raft."

I replied, "Maybe put them in black clothes and lower the lights, use a spotlight on the actors."

He was pissed. "Yup, sure, good point," he muttered.

Our next class was our big scene. We were killing it. The whole class was cracking up. I could feel the high. I knew my teacher would eat his words. He complimented my partner—then turned to me. Took a long pause. And ripped into me. Had me stand on stage while he tore apart everything I did. Even said I held my hand wrong. He shredded me.

But jokes on him. I grew up standing while someone tried to tear me down. If he'd seen my monologue, maybe he'd know that.

The class was silent. Even the theater kids looked more broken than I did. Afterward, they tried to comfort me. "He targeted you!" they said. I appreciated it. But all I could think was: why didn't you stand up for me then?

I finished the semester but didn't continue acting classes. Another trait of mine: when faced with discomfort, instead of valuing myself and pursuing something I might be good at, I bailed. I also didn't see a future in acting. I'd grown up in L.A. I knew what that life was. It was audition after audition, all dependent on others liking you. If I did go that route, I'd rather be a writer.

Eventually, I reconnected with the model guy. We made plans to go to Napa in a hot air balloon. I was excited all week. That same week, I chatted with a woman in the school library about spiritual stuff. I told her we have to live life now. Sitting next to us was a guy I barely noticed. I left the library, and while tying my shoe, saw him again. Long blond hair, big blue eyes. I didn't give it much thought.

For some reason, I left class to get water. Today, everyone's obsessed with hydration—we carry cups and mugs and Stanleys. Back then, it was just a rusty, dusty water fountain. I walked out, and there he was AGAIN. He walked up to me, and I said, "Do I know you?" I was starting to wonder what the hell was going on.

I didn't think I was hot enough for someone to follow me. I had a boyish figure, small chest, no hips, and very little self-worth. But he said, "No, but I heard your conversation about the universe and life, and I wanted to meet you."

He told me his name was Scott and said, "Can I give you my number?" I thought it was cool that he didn't push for mine. I said sure, took the piece of paper, stuffed it away, and figured I'd never call him because I had plans.

That week, Hot Air Balloon Boy never called me. My intuition told me something was up—there was someone else. I didn't know why, I just knew. So I called him. He sounded nervous and said he had to cancel. I could tell it was a lie.

I just said, "Yup, uh huh, sure." I think I even asked, "Is someone there?" I could feel it. Then I hung up. I pulled out Scott's number and said, "Fuck it, let's see what's up with him."

I called him. We went on the best date—chill, low-key, pizza and beer. We talked a ton. He was calming, chill, and I promptly fell in love. And yes, I finally lost my V card—not that night, but not far behind. I was 21, a late bloomer. He was kind, gentle, and we fell in love.

We were together for two years, and then he broke my heart. I wasn't too surprised—I intuitively never saw him as good for my future. He never seemed like someone I could count on. He felt wishy-washy. I wish I had listened to that intuition more in matters of love later in my life.

To be fair, I've learned that intuition sucks in love. That's why readers go to each other when we fall in love—because intuition comes from the heart, and the heart wants what it wants. Once you're in love, you can't discern—is this what I want or what my intuition is telling me?

Later, I found out Hot Air Balloon Boy *did* have someone at his house. Remember, I was friends with his sister. It was his ex. Once she heard about me, she flew in from out of the country to see him. That weekend they reconnected and she got pregnant. And being the good Christian boy he was—he married her.

Remember how I said our decisions are like dominoes? Each one affects the next and changes the future. That's what happened to him. The crazy part was, on the way up to Northern California, I told him, "You seem lost." He said he had a five-year plan for his life and was going to stick to it.

I warned him, "Don't be so rigid. Pay attention to the now. Be flexible. Because if you don't, your life could take a sudden turn and all your plans will fall apart."

He said, "I wish I could understand that. I wish I knew how to live that way."

When I heard what happened to him, I knew—I had seen it. I was warning him. This kind of thing started happening to me a lot in those days, before I even realized I could see possible futures.

The oddest part about all this is who he married looked exactly like me—tall, thin, curly hair. Her name was even similar, which is crazy considering I don't have a common name. Clearly, he had a type. I learned a lot in Northern California, but my sister met someone. I thought about staying there and getting my own apartment, but I missed the creative vibes in L.A., the uniqueness of the people. Los Angeles had the best of everything. One minute, you see a guy running down Hollywood Blvd in a Superman Costume, the next you're hanging with an intellectual at a bookstore. I liked the diversity and open-mindedness. The Bay Area wasn't for me. Don't come for me San Francisco, but you guys can be a little snobby, a little judgy. I was ready for my crazy, artsy, radical L.A., and I decided to come home.

My plan was to go back to my dad's, stay for three months, then leave. Soon after I made these plans, I had an odd interaction. One day, walking in the streets of San Francisco, just a few days before I was set to leave for Los Angeles, I had $450 in cash in my pocket for the trip. This was the early '90s. Debit cards weren't as good, my bank account was usually empty, and overdraft was insane. Cash was still king.

A person walked up to me and said they were from this awesome organization where people connected with each other—a spiritual place where people gathered. Would I like to meet new people? I had been feeling like I had people, or energies, helping and guiding me. I couldn't explain it, but I felt something was there.

I used to take the bus everywhere. I never had a car in the Bay Area. I'd take the bus to my preschool job and always stop at this donut shop. The woman who worked there was so kind. She knew I was broke and always gave me a free donut. We would sit and talk. She'd tell me she had to wake up at 4 a.m. to get to work. I asked her how she stayed so positive, and she'd say she just focused on the good things. I told her, "One day I might be famous." I wasn't saying this for fame's sake—I wanted to be a hero to her, to come back and thank her. "When I do," I said, "I'll come back, remember you, and give you money so you can take a break." She smiled, laughed, and said, "Ok, I believe you."

She had this look in her eyes like, "Aw, she's so cute." But I meant it. I keep track of people who are kind. Angels aren't always mystical beings—they are people here who hold on to their light. I never forgot her. On cold days, she let me sit there and fed me. Isn't that the real Christian way?

One day I was waiting at the bus stop, thinking about how I hated my life. I had a pretty good job, but I was always broke. A decent boyfriend, but I didn't think he really loved me. I liked school but didn't feel connected to it. I was miserable. I got on the bus and sat down. The driver turned to me and said, "You know, if I had your life, I would be happy." I paused. "Excuse me, what?"

He said, "You have a pretty good life." I was stunned. It felt like he read my mind. He wasn't just saying "be happy"—he was speaking to the exact thing I had been thinking. Another time, a bus driver told me she had brain cancer and overcame it. She reminded me to be grateful every day and not to sweat the small stuff.

These drivers were Black, and often in my dreams, the angels that speak to me are Black too. I think it's because of my father and my connection to him. I was so spiritually open during this time. Signs aren't always obvious. They're subtle and don't always come from yogis or pastors. Sometimes they come from a woman giving you a free donut.

So at 23-ish, spiritually wide open, I was walking through my favorite spot in the city: Berkeley. Very hippie, vibey area. I accepted an invitation to a spiritual gathering. A van pulled up, someone hopped out and, in a very relaxed zen tone said, "We can take you there." I looked inside. It was full of cool-looking people, so I said, "Ok," and hopped in.

Before you judge me—yes, I know it sounds insane—but the van wasn't white and windowless. It looked more like a church van. When you come from a cult-like religion, this sort of thing feels weirdly familiar. I was one of those people from church, knocking on strangers' doors to save them. So a group talking about love and harmony didn't feel that foreign.

We didn't go far. Once we arrived, they asked us to remove our shoes. The meeting would take place upstairs. At that moment, I got a slight ping—a sense to leave. But it looked peaceful, so I stayed. We entered a room, they dimmed the lights and played a film. It looked like utopia. The narrator's voice was calming, explaining how we could all live in harmony and love.

Then my little ping turned into an ALARM: "FUCK, THIS IS A CULT." My Nancy experience, my Seventh-day Adventist background—all of it kicked in. I knew I had to get the hell out of there.

When the movie ended, we gathered in a room. Two people started in on me. "How did you like the movie?"

"Fine," I said. "I'm not interested."

They pushed. I noticed one woman eyeing someone like she was getting signals to push harder. She had a hardened, off energy. I could feel it. I kept saying, "Not interested." Then I got up to leave.

They followed me. "Where are my shoes?" I was already mentally preparing to leave in my socks if I had to.

"Don't you want to find enlightenment? We're leaving tonight for a special place," they said. I don't remember the name, but they had one.

"Nope."

One of them got angry. "You're not dedicated to this."

Lady, I just met you! I'm not going to your mystery compound tonight!

I have this inner strength that's always been there—a deep sense of, "I will not be controlled." It kicked in. I bolted. Ran to the nearest phone booth and called my ex-boyfriend.

I told him everything—what happened, where I was, who I met. He yelled, "Oh my God, Adela! Those are the Moonies!"

"What?!"

He explained they were a scary cult. People go to that compound and are never heard from again. A journalist once went undercover and had to escape.

I freaked out. I almost ended up on a cult documentary.

But I also felt validated—I had sensed it. My intuition worked.

A few days later, I left for L.A. I lived with my dad for a few months and got a job at a dollar movie theater. The vibes were very Gen X. I saw *Clerks* there and thought, "This is us."

I stayed quiet about my spiritual side, trying to live a "normal" life.

About six months later, I met a guy at the store next to the theater. Rocker type. Long hair. We hit it off, and on our first date he told me his sister had been killed nine months earlier. I now realize we trauma-bonded over grief. He told me about his mom, who went to psychics and mediums.

This drew me in. I met her, and she was normal—not weirded out by my experiences. In fact, she was curious and encouraging. I started reading for her. I won't share those readings out of respect, but she helped me, and later she told me I had helped her.

At that time, I was still very much in the closet about my gifts. I saw myself as a medium, not an intuitive yet.

We moved in together. We cared for each other, but it was never romantic. Still, he and his mom are a huge part of my spiritual path.

What shoved me all the way into it was when I started working at a small coffee company that had just come to L.A.

I got the job, and I was part of the crew to open their 5th shop in Los Angeles.

That company?

Starbucks.

And it would change my life forever.

Chapter Six
Starbucks Saves Me

Once upon a time, long, long ago, before people ever heard of the name Starbucks, the green mermaid landed here in Los Angeles. They were still pretty new to the world. I was hired to open the 5th Starbucks in Los Angeles, located in Studio City on the corner of Vineland & Laurel Canyon. I always loved the smell of coffee. My grandmother—my mother's mom—lived with us and she would sneak me a little bit of her coffee.

It was the '90s, and coffee shops were all the rage, especially here in L.A. I heard of this new company called Starbucks, and they were progressive. They offered benefits for only 25-hour work weeks, free coffee beans each week, and they paid more than the previous coffee shop I worked at. They promised stock options. It seemed different, more organized—like a real company, in COFFEE, which was still a new concept. Up till then, it was just small little coffee shops.

I was against corporate jobs and never had any desire to climb a corporate ladder, but Starbucks wasn't those things... yet. I needed insurance. I needed stability. So I signed up— and I landed the job. My manager seemed cool. He had long hair, was a skinny guy, and looked more like a chill hippie. He later told me his plan was to put together an interesting crew. He did that. And 30 years later, we still know each other. Shout out to the OG crew!

I was still on my spiritual quest, practicing readings with my then-boyfriend's mother. I started to read a book about a famous medium who spoke of his journey, but mostly it was a transcript of his readings. I really didn't know what I thought about it—I was still a skeptic myself. My boyfriend's mom, Maxine, was so supportive. I loved how she accepted me. She was from the South, but open-minded. She wasn't the usual type you'd expect to be into psychics. Honestly, it's why I trusted her more.

So now I had a job and sort of a path. I went to Starbucks school. They used to have one tucked away behind another store on Vineland, located in Sherman Oaks, just down the street from the one we were opening. We learned the drinks—how to call them. Back then it was basic drinks: drip coffee, latte, mocha, cappuccino, espresso shot—you get the picture. Basic. Maybe five syrups. Not the Starbucks you see today. We learned how to hand-make EVERYTHING. That was how it was. We learned about coffee—where it came from, the difference between a Kenya bean and a Colombian bean. In those days, it was all about the brew, roast, the purity of coffee. Today it's all about iced coffee and how many flavors you can add to it.

We had huge bean drawers filled with coffee beans where we scooped fresh beans every day and ground them for daily coffee. We also sold coffee beans and did taste tests for customers. It was run similar to a winery.

After we were all trained at Starbucks School, we were getting ready for our grand opening. I remember lining up in those green aprons—they were so long I rolled mine up to make them look cute. We lined up like soldiers, side by side, ready for our fearless leader—the district manager and our store manager—standing in front. People were peeking in, trying to get in, seeing if we were open. Since there weren't a lot of Starbucks stores then, people were excited.

Today, I can throw a stone and hit a Starbucks just around me. (This is a good commercial for Starbucks—hit me up SB, I'll partner brand with you!)

We had no idea the insanity that was waiting for us. Our district manager looked at us and said, "This store is going to be the busiest store we have ever opened and the most demanding customers we have ever had." He went on to explain, "We're in the heart of the studios, where they film shows like *Seinfeld* and *Friends*. So many famous people live in this area—and directors, heads of studios, etc."

I remember thinking, *What is this? I thought it was just coffee?!* This felt like some revolution—and well… it was!

We opened, and the insanity was like we were rock stars. Customers stared at us as we flung coffee. Honestly, I could do a whole book on the beginning years of Starbucks. At least a documentary should be done. My friend Jeff and I even recorded a podcast for a short time called *When Starbucks Was Fun*. We'll circle back to Jeff soon.

However, this chapter, although dedicated to Starbucks and how it changed my life—and my love for coffee—is not just about that. This was before the internet and social media, so the phenomenon was beyond anything we realized. People would recognize us on the street. Those days, Starbucks was *the* place to be and to be seen.

I do credit my manager Tony—he deserves a shout-out! He made it a fun place to work, even with all the stress. He always stayed calm and never yelled or belittled us. He helped create the success of...

The store ranked in the top five nationally in sales! I thought my manager was way older than me—later I realized he was in his mid-twenties. So there we were, all in our twenties, helping this company become a billion-dollar success. And believe me, we did help them become just that. Like I said, there should be a documentary about those days.

I had no patience for customers—they were demanding, rude, and carried huge L.A. privileged attitudes. Not the celebrities, surprisingly. They weren't rude—maybe a few times. Once, Jim Carrey came in at the height of his career and went straight to the front of the line. He told Alex, who was the cashier at the time, "I'm a millionaire, I don't wait in line." He handed him a wad of cash and said, "Pay for everyone behind me," and tipped the crew big! Today, that would be all over TikTok.

It was the wannabe-famous types that were the worst—the ones dying to be famous, like the PAs (production assistants). To be fair, they were treated horribly on the shows they worked on, but still. It was the era of rag mags, and they always took pictures of celebs leaving Starbucks holding their cups. Wide shot of the logo front and center—it was brilliant marketing. Holding a Starbucks cup back then was a kind of status symbol.

My strength turned out to be that I was fast on bar, which surprised me! Not so much on the cash register. I had a reputation for being sort of bitchy, standoffish, and intimidating. I wasn't much of a company woman and didn't drink the corporate Kool-Aid Starbucks was handing out. I saw they were a growing company making money off of us, and my spiritual side was bothered by that. I was "woke" before people even said those words. I was aware. And although I appreciated them and how progressive they were—and I did love being a part of it—I mostly kept to myself.

Like many of us in my generation, I was broken, damaged, but never got help. Mental health wasn't something anyone talked about. So we laughed, had fun, bonded. But we never talked about our trauma. We all had so much going on, but no one really shared. I had lost my mom a few years ago, went through the Nancy saga, and my father wasn't there for me at the time. I felt alone, lost, sad. I was working with kids in preschool as well—two jobs.

For the boomers who called us lazy and slackers—most of us Gen Xers were hustlers. I was on my spiritual journey, and although I was practicing all the time with Maxine, I felt it was time to practice on a stranger.

I worked nights, mostly closing shifts. I was the best damn closer because of my years growing up cleaning and cooking, taking care of my family. I think this gave me a leg up on how to get shit done.

Jeff—told you I'd get back to him—had started working nights. He was bright, positive, had long hair, and was openly gay, which in the early 90s was not easy at all. As a matter of fact, we had a lot of openly gay men working at Starbucks. Shout out to Starbucks for being LGBTQ+ friendly and one of the first companies to offer domestic partner insurance.

I point this out because although Jeff was open and friendly, I hardly knew anything about him. He had just started, but I heard he had recently lost his father. We didn't share our personal problems or emotional pains in those days. Shoving all that shit down was considered strong and brave. Showing emotions and sadness was considered weak. Raise your hand if you were raised by boomers.

Our therapy was listening to loud music in our cars, screaming and crying there. We used to actually blast Rage Against the Machine while closing the store at night. Those days, it wasn't nearly as corporate as today. We did our own thing, blasted Nine Inch Nails' "Closer," and got out all our angst while we cleaned and stocked.

One day I decided that Jeff would be the perfect first stranger to practice on. I had a plan—if I could read a stranger I knew nothing about, maybe this shit was real.

So I pulled up one day and I heard a man in my mind's eye—though in those days I didn't even know that term. I heard him say, "He's working today." Jeff didn't always close—his shiny personality was more fitting for the morning. The voice said, "Please talk to him."

I was terrified. My heart was pounding. I didn't know Jeff, and later Jeff told me he was scared of little old me! Understandable. I laugh out loud as I type this—I was in so much pain, but my pain came out as anger instead of vulnerability. He told me that people warned him to stay out of my way—that I was sort of a bitch.

I feel sad for that twenty-something girl. She wanted to be understood, loved, maybe even make friends. I was just and sad, broken—and the most sensitive people usually put up the strongest armor. They're also the ones who cry alone.

I argued with the voice. I said, "Nope, he usually doesn't work this time."

The voice disagreed. "Please talk to him."

I walked in... and yup, there was Jeff—smiling, cheerful. He had just lost his father and still had a wonderful attitude. I look back and realize maybe he too was covering his pain.

I promptly walked right by. "Not today."

But that did prove to me the voice was real. I needed confirmation, and that is something I still use to this day.

The next time I worked, I don't remember the day, but I pulled up and heard the voice again: "He's here."

I argued again, but the beat in my chest was strong. I had to decide—okay, this is the day. I walked in. Jeff was there. I waited until my break. Jeff was on till (cashier). I walked right up to him and said:

"So... you might think I'm nuts, and it's okay if you say 'fuck you' or whatever, but does your father look like this?"

I described him. His dad did not look like Jeff to me—his father's hair was balding, missing, and darker. Jeff had long, blond, thick hair.

He looked at me and smiled. "Yes."

"That's him. What is he saying?"

I was horrified—I really didn't expect him to agree. I was stunned. I was also annoyed, and I asked him if he was okay with any of this. I said it in a tone that was almost like, "WTF, why are you okay with this?" He said, "Yes, I'm into things like this."

I told him I had to go and ran out to my car, where I lit a cigarette and sat there smoking, muttering to myself, "What is happening? How am I hearing this?" It felt like I was in one of those movies where someone discovers they have some kind of power or gift that starts emerging out of nowhere.

Then I heard the voice again: "You've been tapped. This is your gift. Here are the rules: Do not use any words but mine. Don't get an ego about this—it's not about you, it's about us and them. Also, be humble."

I finished my cigarette, walked back inside, and found Jeff still at the register. He turned to me, waiting for more. I said, "Okay, well... your father is a gentle man."

Then I paused, second-guessing myself. I thought, how stupid. Everyone who dies gets remembered as a hero or a gentle soul. So I corrected myself: "Sorry, maybe that's wrong. Everyone is like this."

Jeff paused from what he was doing, looked directly into my eyes, and said, "Listen, on my father's tombstone, we wrote 'HE WAS A GENTLE MAN.' You are correct."

Again, I freaked out. I was happy because I saw I had connected to something—but I was also shocked and almost disappointed. What was I supposed to do now?

I said, "Okay, wow, I'll be back." And ran to my car again, lit another cigarette, and listened. This time, I tuned in more clearly and received more messages. I went back inside and conveyed them to Jeff.

Back on shift, I told Jeff that his father wanted him to live his life and be free. He went on to say he wished he had told Jeff this before he died—he was referring to Jeff coming out. Jeff confirmed that yes, they had found a letter after his father passed, saying all those things.

I was more upset that I was right. It meant this was real.

Jeff, meanwhile, was more of a believer than I was.

At one point, I turned to Jeff and said, "Your father says, 'Live your fucking life.'"

Immediately, I heard a loud correction: "NO! I NEVER CURSED!"

His father added, "Remember the rules: only use my words! Only speak what I tell you!"

I felt a little taken aback—like, who is this guy to make demands of me? But instead, I turned to Jeff and conveyed exactly what his dad had said. Jeff laughed and confirmed, "Nope, he never did."

We bonded after that. I've had a connection to Jeff ever since. I always considered his father my first teacher. From that point on, everything I learned came from the other side.

Starbucks saved me because it gave me a place to come out of the mediumship closet. I realized things about myself, made some real friends, was part of pop culture history, and learned how to stay true to myself while still working for "the man."

After that day, there was no denying who I was.

I later met Jeff's mom. She was kind and thankful for the readings I did. I had mixed feelings—I was embarrassed but also so grateful for her acceptance and kindness.

I went on to try reading other people everywhere I went.

Another major life event happened at Starbucks: I met my first husband. I wish I could say this was a good thing. It wasn't. I ended up shutting all my spiritual gifts down after I met him—with his encouragement—and went back into the broom closet.

But my gifts would save me yet again.

P.S. Starbucks, call me!

Chapter Seven
Intuition & The Escape

My boyfriend and I broke up rather quickly. We made better friends than romantic partners. I moved out and still remained close to his mother—she did change my life, and I loved her very much.

Months before that, I had decided I wanted to start bartending. If I was a good barista, I'd probably make a good bartender—was my logic. So I signed up for bartending school, which is sort of a scam, but there weren't any tutorial videos on YouTube… yet. People kept telling me I could learn on the job, but because I didn't drink much, I felt better taking a class. My knowledge of drinking was rum and coke, so mixed drinks, wine, and beer—I wasn't familiar with. No one drank in my house growing up. The first time I was around anyone drinking was at a party with the kids from my Waldorf school.

The class was in North Hollywood and our teacher had a tough exterior vibe and a no-bullshit attitude. She was a little rough around the edges and looked like she smoked her whole life. At the time, I thought she was way older than me, but she was probably more like thirty years old. She wasn't the usual type of person you'd see in Los Angeles. Most people here are pretty refined and self-conscious. She had a tone to her that rang, "I don't give a shit what you think. Fuck everybody!" I liked it—and her. Plus, she really did take this class seriously.

The room was set up like a mock bar, which was very familiar to me—similar to Starbucks and the mock coffee shop. She had bottles with liquid that clearly had water with food coloring to make it look like rum, whiskey, vodka. She had all the glasses. I think I borrowed the money from my sister Laurie, and I was convinced this was the answer to make money. My plan was to learn how to bartend so I could quit Starbucks and work full-time as a bartender.

Learning the drinks was similar to being a barista. Once you learned basic recipes, it was easy to learn the rest. For example, a screwdriver is vodka and orange juice—switch out cranberry and you got a vodka cranberry. Switch out the cranberry, add grapefruit, and you have a greyhound. I loved making drinks—it's almost like potions to me. Whether it's coffee or alcohol, it's all alchemy. I took to it pretty well and graduated. Received my certificate—look out world!

I really thought having this certificate would make a difference and open doors. Our teacher left out that no one gave a shit. I guess that would be bad for business! I wasn't a fast-slinging bartender and women bartenders weren't easily hired then. My friends wanted me to work at a lesbian bar, but I felt wrong tricking people and acting flirty for tips. So I ended up at a restaurant. It was somewhat corporate—like Starbucks—but for Mexican food.

I was at the bar making margaritas, having men sit there talking to me, thinking I was their friend or hoping for more. It was pretty tame and I don't think I sold the look of nightlife. People always saw the innocence in me. I liked making tips. I liked that all I had to do was mix simple drinks—it was way easier than Starbucks. I could pop a cap off a bottle of beer and get tipped a dollar. Getting tipsy makes people more happy than coffee. I disagree, sitting here now with my coffee beside me. Tip your baristas, people.

The bar area was okay. The only nice touch was the bar top—it was made out of copper. It was a bitch to clean and I can still smell it. The bar top didn't lift, so I had to hunch down and crawl under a small opening, and at 5'11, it was not easy. My knees have never been the same.

I was now working at Starbucks and at The Crocodile Café. I moved home right after I broke up with my ex. Before I got the job at Crocodile Café, I had put the word out that I was looking for a bartending job. One day, a customer came to Starbucks. I mentioned it to him and of course he offered his help. So nice of him, helping a young, pretty girl. (Insert eye roll.) I believed he really wanted to help me—at first. I forgot he gave me his number. I was thinking of calling, but something in me said to wait.

In the meantime, I was practicing reading other people. After Jeff, I wanted to see who else. What I didn't know then—it was important to ask permission from people, not just go up and read them.

I had a friend from The Crocodile Café. We sometimes talked. He wasn't into me at all. He was bragging about being an ex-Satanist and at the time I started to pick up tarot cards. So I practiced on him. He was cool about it, so it felt safe. Once, we went out to eat. While we were eating, I told him I saw a woman behind him. She was older? Maybe his grandmother? I asked him if his grandmother passed. He was in the middle of pouring sugar into his tea and froze! He slowly looked up: "Why are you saying this?"

I tried to tell him how I can communicate to spirits. He confirmed his grandmother died—all while he was still frozen, staring at me. I said, "Oh, she pats you on your head. Says 'my baby.'" He freaks out and says she did that all the time and she raised him. He told me to stop. I apologized and realized I shouldn't have done that.

Another time at work I did the same to a server. She came up to the bar to get her drink, I gave it to her, and started saying things about her father. She freaks out and asks me how I know these things!! I asked her if her dad died and she says, "NO! HE'S ALIVE, BUT WE HAVEN'T TALKED!"

I stopped. I apologized and never brought it up again, but I also realized—my gifts changed! Or grew! How did I see an alive person?

Another time at Starbucks I did the same thing to someone I sort of knew. His dad had died a while ago. I tuned into him and saw his dad and proceeded to give him my description of him and how his dad felt about him when he was alive. It was accurate, but he was so freaked out and demanded I stop.

At Starbucks they started making fun of me, calling me weirdo and witch. I should've taken it as a compliment—but I didn't.

The bartending job—they didn't care much. They treated me like they couldn't be bothered. Most of them were high on coke. Really common in restaurant jobs, especially in L.A. So I think their attention span was short. Luckily for me.

The reason I teach today and mentor people, and created a podcast, and put out content online—and why I am even writing this book—is because I want to hopefully help anyone who is scared to embrace who they are. Doesn't matter in what way—spiritually or mundanely—it's a horrible feeling to have to hide yourself.

Despite that I had a strong feeling and message from somewhere to stay at my father's, get myself together, and focus on me—not date anyone—I ignored my intuition and called the guy who said he'd help me get a job.

When I met—let's call him Bob (I want to give him the most basic name; no offense to the Bobs in the world, but his real name is also pretty basic)—he wasn't. I was very much on the fence about my gifts. What to do with them? Are they real? Are they dangerous? I was vulnerable, lost.

When I went home to my dad's, it was always with the intention to leave quickly. I felt uncomfortable at his house—it was awkward—and at the same time, I told him everything. Too much pain in that house. Too much pain with him. So when I came home, I heard something speaking to me telepathically, telling me to stay put, to not get involved with anyone, to honor peace. I did feel peaceful for a while—for the first time in a long time. I think that scared me. I was used to chaos and pain. So when I called Bob and he asked me on a date—what did I do? I went. I found my little black dress and went.

We met at a Mexican bar called El Coyote in Hollywood. Unlike my bar, this was a cool place. I walked in and saw him—he definitely was handsome, looked like a young Billy Dee Williams.

I sat down and I knew immediately he was not good for me. I knew his energy felt off. I believe he was late, actually. The version I just told you was how I wanted to see myself. Here's the real story: he was a half-hour late—so I left. Yes, good job, Adela!

If I was watching the movie of me, I'd say, damn good boundaries, girl! He called and apologized, and that dumb young girl went back thinking I really did something. I knew even then, before I saw him, this was bad. He was charming, cocky, and I found out on the date he was 13 years my senior—it freaked me out a little. I was now about 24; he was about 37. He looked a lot younger. So I stayed to see where this would go.

I feel so bad for her—that young girl. No one really to help her that she trusted. To warn her. This is why I do this work I do: to guide and help anyone avoid the hard lessons I lived.

We do have choices, and those choices determine our future. I don't believe the only way to learn is through pain. I don't believe in "it was meant to be." Every decision falls upon other decisions and therefore the future can be changed. I wish I had an Adela to warn me about this path.

I know what you're thinking—I wouldn't listen. You're wrong. Because I didn't listen to those who hurt me or didn't have my back or accept me. If I had a kind person like Maxine who would accept me, I definitely would have had a fighting chance.

People want help—they just want it with acceptance of who they are, as long as someone isn't hurting or abusing anyone. Consenting adults—people should be allowed to live however they want.

I called a friend after that date and told her, "Yeah, he's cocky, he's rude. I'm done with him." She was an accepting friend and was kind, but we weren't super close. She listened, agreed—and I promptly went out with him again.

Here is the thing about intuition and love: it doesn't work once you're bitten, smitten. It won't work once you fall down that rabbit hole. It does work when you first go on a date—that first hit on someone is always right. However, you have to listen to it.

Once I let my first wall down, it's over. Intuition comes from the heart, and the heart wants what it wants. Therefore, you're screwed once the heart is attached. This is why us readers get readings from each other for matters of the heart.

I dated him. Five years later, I married him in an awful, horrible court wedding.

It was the worst relationship I could imagine—verbally abusive. We went homeless together, which, by the way, I think he liked. I stopped trying to pursue any bartending job, and with his encouragement, I closed myself off from my gifts.

I was working at Starbucks still, and I helped open a new Hollywood location. It was one of the first to land directly in Hollywood. I worked with a great new manager! No one knew I was sleeping in my car with Bob. I didn't have to sleep in my car—it was by choice. My family would have taken me in. I had it in my head he needed me. It was us against the world.

I am not going to write every detail of this time—I'm writing more about my gifts: how they came into play and how I muted them.

When I met him, I told him about my gifts. I told him I felt there was like a cloud around me that I couldn't see. I knew it had to do with my abilities. I wasn't sure if I believed in God or what, and at that time I interpreted it as bad. It felt like something trying to connect. He told me I should shut it all down and not use it again.

I listened. And for five years, I muted my gifts. I ignored my intuition. It's kind of like someone having this superpower, and the villain comes along and convinces them, "Yes, it's bad. Don't use that."

We moved to the Midwest, where he was from. When I say moved, I mean this was after we went homeless. We left Los Angeles, then moved to Vegas for three years. He actually worked—a little, very little. He didn't have a drinking or gambling problem; he hardly did either. Later I would surmise he had severe mental health issues.

I wish I had the internet then like we do today. Wish I had social media or Google. I probably would have left him long ago.

We moved from Vegas to Seattle. He obtained a job there. In Vegas, they only had one Starbucks on the Strip, and of course that's where I worked. Starbucks allows you to transfer from store to store. After he secured a job in Seattle, we then moved.

Seattle felt like heaven after Vegas. Beautiful.

Water and trees—I fell in love. It was a breath of literal fresh air. Living in Vegas felt like hell; there was no way to really feel my spiritual self. Bob was an interesting man—smart, handsome, had a good sense of humor. At the time, that's what I saw. I didn't recognize his mental health issues because my compassion for the pain he had gone through as a child blinded me. The downside to being intuitive is your compassionate heart.

Ironically, where Starbucks originated in Seattle, I did not work there. Instead, I worked at a private school as a teacher's assistant. We ran out of money because his job wasn't very stable—mostly due to his paranoia—so we sold everything and moved to the Midwest to live with his family. They owned a family business and sometimes we would go there so he could make some money. But we would always leave again—he was too paranoid about his family, so it never lasted.

This time, things were different. I started to feel different about him. I started to follow my intuition. In the past, whenever we stayed with his family, he never liked me getting a job. He didn't want to settle. This time, I ignored him. I got a little coffee job and started squirreling money away from my tips. He didn't know. I know now it sounds like an abused, controlled wife planning her escape. I didn't fully see it that way... yet. He never hit me, but the abuse was mental and verbal.

He also thought it was my job to cater to him—cook for him, wash his back. So who cared what he thought? I met a really nice woman at the coffee shop where I worked. She was older, married, had a daughter—the nicest people. One day I told her the truth about my situation, and she said, "Listen, I have an attic you can stay in for free—just give me the word."

She had that look of a woman who.. knew....what she was looking at. I told her thank you, and I'd take her up on it, but when I called, I wanted it to be for real. I had threatened to leave him many times and always went back. This time I was awake. My intuition was on fire. I felt change. I no longer saw him as helpless. He stopped showering, changing his clothes—it was clear he had mental health issues.

I won't get into his family, but to be fair, they didn't know all of this was going on. He wouldn't let me tell them anything. One day, I had it. I made that call.

"Judy, I'm ready. Is that space still available?"

She said, "Of course, but I have to clean it."

"I don't care," I told her. "I'll clean it. I have to leave now."

I went to her house to help clean. I had no idea about attics—we don't have them in California. It was amazing! Two bedrooms. The bathroom had a clawfoot bathtub. HUGE. She told me I could stay there for free. I said no. She said, "Okay, $200." I was so touched. I hugged her and cried.

There are angels in life, but they don't need wings—just compassion and empathy.

I had started a different job by then. I told Bob I was leaving. He laughed, then yelled, then asked to see a movie. I said sure—but I'm still leaving and taking the car. The one I paid for. He tried all the tactics. I didn't budge.

The next day, he took off and called me from a pay phone. Said he was leaving. Said he was on a train. I was so happy. I said, "Okay, but you still have to sign the divorce papers."

He said I was being followed by a spy and hung up.

I finally told his family what had happened. I could finally fill them in. From his siblings, I gathered this wasn't new. He had a history of mental health problem. It started to make sense. I thought back to the time he said our house in Seattle was bugged. The time he thought the president was talking directly to him through the TV. The time he told me I had a chip in my brain and was being controlled.

It's also why it was hard to leave him—knowing he wasn't well. His sister said, "You stayed way longer than I would have." She wished me luck. But they didn't help me. I moved out in the snow, alone, with two cats. And I was grateful I didn't have a kid with him. I'll credit him—he knew that was a bad idea. But it wasn't hard; we never slept together.

I packed up and left. Went to my new home. It was a haven.

He didn't ruin me for life. But he did break me a bit. The trauma and abuse changed something in me that would take years to heal—and I'm still healing.

There are angels that don't have wings. And devils that don't have horns. Devils see your weakness and use it for their own gain—and sometimes relish in the control they have over you.

I heard he came back. One day I was driving home and saw him, standing at a bus stop. This man used to make me take the bus to work in 15 inches of snow while he had the car and sat at home. He expected me to stop. I drove right past him, laughing and waving.

I kept going. The look on his face was worth it.

I heard he left town again. One day his parents called to ask me if I knew where he was. I told them I never heard from him again and wanted nothing to do with him.

You know when you break up with someone and you want closure? I never, ever felt that way. I'm the type of person who tells someone, over and over, "The way you're treating me is killing this." I give people a long rope, with high compassion. I try to understand that life isn't perfect.

But when I'm done, I'm done.

And they're always surprised.

Know this: compassion and empathy take strength. Anyone can choose the path of coldness—that's easy. Keeping your heart open? That's the hard part.

Long ago, at my second preschool job, I worked with some bitter, cold older women. I was 21 and in love for the first time. They kept making fun of me, saying things like, "Oh, wait till you get a divorce. Wait until you're older."

At that moment, I promised myself: I will never become that woman.

I will encourage younger women. Help them. Keep my heart open. It's why I worked with children—they kept the light on in me.

So when I left this man—the one who treated me worse than anyone I'd ever dated—I made a decision. He broke me inside. But I would not grow bitter.

I stayed in the Midwest to heal. I started a new job, and I only got that job because of my intuition. I was springing back to life. I started having visions again.

This vision—this intuition—was leading me to New York. I'd always wanted to live there. And they say you should live in New York at least once.

I was now in my early 30s, starting over. I was scared, happy, ready, and fully awake.

And New York was on my mind.

Chapter Eight
The Narrow Room

While I was going through all this with Bob back in December of 1999, my father passed. I had a feeling while I was living in Vegas that he might've been reaching his end. He was 60, which is young—but not if you've been on dialysis for about 33 years of your life. That's like living to 90 for a healthy person.

I started calling my dad from Vegas every week. We'd talk for hours. I called collect because I couldn't afford to go home. Vegas wasn't far, but we had a junk car and I was living paycheck to paycheck, so it wasn't easy. I think the real reason was because I wasn't in a healthy state of mind or relationship.

This was the first time I lived far from him. My siblings didn't live in L.A.—some were in the O.C., others in Northern California. I kept having this feeling he was dying. I remember once taking a shuttle to one of the casinos—Vegas living means you learn all the hacks to getting around free. There was this older Black man whose skin looked like brand new. I was still very open to my spiritual side, I just pushed it down around Bob.

This man talked about losing his wife. He had dark sunglasses on—similar to the ones my dad used to wear. He reminded me of my father. I felt like he was giving me a message. He was telling me to enjoy life in the moment, to love the people around you now. I told him about my dad. He said, "Call him." Then he got on his shuttle and rode away. I remember thinking this was clearly a message. Once again—at a bus stop. Maybe buses represent crossing of time?

I did call him. I asked him to tell me all about his life again. He seemed bothered and asked why I was asking. I said, "I don't know—I just want to hear your story again." It was like he knew that I knew. He might be dying.

I had shut down my gifts because Bob told me to. But you can't completely shut them off—you can only turn them down.

A week later, I got a call from home. My father had been rushed to the hospital and was declining fast. My brother was calm and logical. He didn't feel I needed to rush home. I trusted him, but my sister was very upset. It was hours before they called my work at the preschool.

My brother told me to come home—they'd pay for the flight. I was going alone—of course not with Bob. I flew out, and by the time I got there, just like with my mother, he was in a coma.

Before my mother died, I asked her, "How long will Dad live without you?"

She said, "Ten years at the most."

My mom died in November of 1989. He was in a coma December of 1999. It had been ten years.

Now I was 29. Somehow, calmer this time. I saw my father in a coma and told my family, "He's not done." They all thought I was crazy. I kept seeing his spirit, and it was turning around every time I called to it. I had no idea why I knew things, but my gifts were perking up again. Like I said—you can turn them down, not off. My family called it that juju thing I did.

One day, my family went to dinner after days of being at the hospital. The hospital let us stay in rooms reserved for pediatric parents—they were empty and they knew who my dad was. His old doctor, Dr. A, was very well known in nephrology. When he walked in, the staff recognized him from their medical school textbooks. Their attitude changed quickly.

I was in the lobby with my sister Laurie (my biological sister). I told her what I saw. She said, "I don't believe in God that way." I mean—I didn't either, but I understood what she meant.

Then suddenly, a nurse came rushing toward me. My heart dropped. I thought, "Okay—I'll be the only one here when he dies." She said, "He is up! Asking for a pen!"

What no one knew was that I kept telling my dad, "Come back—we need you to tell us what you want done with your stuff. You didn't write anything down." I told him this every day in his coma. Telepathically.

When the nurse told me that, I knew. I knew my father heard me.

When everyone got back from dinner, they were all shocked. My other sister said, "Why was it you? Why were you here?"

I didn't really know what she meant—why me? I didn't care. I thought of my weirdness and this gift. Three years before, I had called every family member and told them I had a vision—my father would die in three years. I've since learned I can't see those visions for just anyone. My father's life affected my path. The universe allowed me to see it—same with my mom.

My family did remember I had told them. They said maybe they should have listened.

It's okay. I get it. It's weird and hard to face. But that didn't change the ongoing feeling I had of never being accepted or heard.

My father lived for a month after that. He died on New Year's Eve, December 31st, 1999. We were with him. We decided not to resist his heart. When they took him off life support, I felt him leave. I walked over, felt his forehead, kissed it—he was still warm. I whispered goodbye and told him I loved him.

I have predicted both my parents' deaths. It's not the best place to be in. They say heavy is the head that wears the crown, heavy is the one who sees the future too.

After my dad died, two things happened that had a profound effect on me. The first was when we went to his house. I slept in his bed. My family was weirded out by this. I had a dream that night that I was walking down a long hall and saw a flashing light—I thought it was a TV playing. I kept hearing someone say, "My baby girl, my baby girl." I slowly followed the light and the voice, rounded a corner, and then another booming voice said, "Too far!" I woke up suddenly, gasping for air. I knew it was my dad. He always called me his baby girl.

I used to talk to my dad about my beliefs. He didn't believe in life after death—he was an Adventist. They believe when you die, you die. This reminded me of the dreams I had after my mother died.

Back around 1989, I was sharing a room and bed with my sister and her baby. We had gone from a six-bedroom house to a small two-bedroom townhome. I was sleeping, hanging onto my corner of the bed, when I heard a sound of wind come through the window, which was odd because we never slept with it open. I was paralyzed and couldn't move. Sleep paralysis was familiar to me—something I had since I was a kid, but I didn't know the name of this phenomenon back then, just the experience. I was laying there and could see the wall to my right. I was paralyzed but awake. Sounds like a horror movie. I wasn't scared, but my eyes were open, and then I heard the sound of wind move toward my bed.

Sitting on my bed was my mom. She was in the same nightgown I was used to seeing her wear my whole life. Sounds cliché, but she wore long white nightgowns every night. She said, "You're okay. Your father is okay." I told her she died and that Daddy was depressed and I was worried. She said, "It's okay, he'll be okay," and then she was gone. I was released from the paralysis and I jumped up. I looked at the window—it was closed. I felt confused and so sad. How did this happen and why didn't she say more?

My sister was asleep. I walked around the townhome looking for her. It felt so real I swore she was there. I had no idea how this happened—how did I see her so clearly? How did I feel wind? Why couldn't I move? Was it real? Was it in my mind only? Was it made up by grief? Something deep in my heart and mind knew it was real. She finally spoke, or I finally could hear her. I didn't tell my sister. I didn't tell anyone. I just kept that to myself.

Once I started to accept that I was able to see and hear from my mom, I started to have several experiences. Around Christmas time, growing up, our family celebrated Kwanzaa, not Christmas. Since my mom passed, like most families, when the glue of the family is gone, the celebrations change. We didn't start celebrating Christmas, but we went up to my brother's house, who lived near Napa. He had just gotten married. I can't remember why we were there exactly, but I do remember a specific dream.

I dreamed that I walked up to my mom and she was sitting in a small room. It reminded me of a box. She was sad and looked different, maybe younger. I've since learned over the years that spirits often come to you looking younger because age doesn't matter in that realm. Appearance in general is not important. Since spirits are just energy, they can change their look to anything they want—think like an online avatar. Some spirits will appear in their twenties or thirties—whatever age they liked.

So when I saw my mom, I didn't care about all that. I just saw her. I walked up to her. I said, "Mom, why are you sad?" She said, "Because no one's talking to me. No one seems to realize I am here." I told her, "I do. I am talking to you." She dropped her head and I could feel her energy drop and she replied, "You're the only one."

I had this feeling in the dream as though I didn't understand why she felt this way. I felt in some way she was mistaken—almost like, oh this is some error. Of course they would love to talk to you. I must run and fix this. Maybe there was just some miscommunication.

I bolted out to tell my family. I was so happy and excited to do so. I ran out and said, "I had a dream about Mommy and she's sad that no one is talking to her or about her." They all just froze. Said nothing. I understand it's painful and I also understand they didn't really believe me. I felt alone in grief and, once again, misunderstood. Another reason I felt the need to just shut up. That's the curse of this gift.

One night I had another unique dream with my mom. She showed me all the ways she tried to speak to different family members. She showed me how my sister was struggling, trying to fill my mom's shoes. She showed me Tanya talking to a cousin of ours about this very subject. Then the scene changed to my brother Jared. She said he was deciding to take a job position he thought she would approve of—that he was considering taking the job offer for her, to make her happy. She also told me she tried to talk to him while he slept. He would toss and turn and sort of hear her, but she didn't think he really heard her. Lastly, she showed me my older brother Aub. Sadly, she said, "He doesn't hear me at all. He's totally blocked and I can't get through."

I woke up suddenly, gasping for air. I knew this was another message and visit. I wasn't excited to call my sister, but I was hopeful. Maybe she'd get it?

From past experiences, I learned that if I had dreams like this, I needed to share them. Sometimes they are full premonitions. Sometimes I'm just seeing into people's lives. Remote viewing them. Either way, I have learned not to ignore my dreams.

I called my sister. I told her everything. There was a long pause. Then she said, "Well, I don't know how you know these things. I did have a conversation regarding Mommy. We did discuss exactly what you are saying." She went on to tell me my brother was deciding to take a job and had told my sister he wished he could talk to our mom. She said, "I'm not sure how you know this," and her tone was guarded and unsure.

At the time, I felt hurt and disappointed. Today, I understand it more. I hung up not feeling validated, but I did it—at least I passed the message on.

For my budding intuitives and mediums: don't read friends and family. Especially if they didn't ask. It's too jarring and can ruin relationships.

Rule of thumb: always ask permission first.

Now 10 years later after several experiences and dreams like this I knew my dad WAS talking to me. I used to tell him about the dreams I had about my mom and he would joke about it a lot. "So are they watching me when I shower?" he'd laugh. He always acted like he didn't believe, but when I asked him if he ever had a near-death experience, he said he did.

After my dad passed we had a memorial honoring him at his church. We called it A Celebration of Life. I loved the concept and thought it was so different. My dad came from Detroit and he wanted a traditional funeral service, but because my mom was cremated, he chose to do the same. I decided I wanted to speak at his memorial. The night before, I wrote something. I didn't know what to write but I felt him. I could feel his energy. I felt a surge of love and this feeling overtook me. I needed to write it down. I grabbed a pen and paper and I felt this message come through me.

The next day at the memorial so many people said wonderful things—it was standing room only. His friends, family, his students, even the doctors and nurses, all spoke. The choir sang beautifully and someone performed one of his favorite hymns. Even though I did not like church, I loved this for him. When it was my turn to speak, my heart was pounding. I started to wonder why did I agree to this? But I felt an urge, a need beyond myself, and I wanted to deliver the message I felt my dad wanted everyone to hear.

This is what I wrote:

The Gift: The Gift my father gave you was his pain. The Gift my father gave you was his faith. My father's life gave you so many gifts, willingly, freely, and purely! Please leave here today taking one of these gifts and remember that my father never was and never is about Death! If you asked him what he was so happy about, he'd say with a boom in his voice LIFE! When you leave here today, put in your pockets one, if not all, of these Gifts. Go home and live each day like my father. When I would see my father each morning, I would see him smiling with such a shine in his eyes. I'd say, "Daddy, what are you smiling about?" And he'd say, with his fist held high in the air, "LIFE, LIFE, LIFE!"

I looked up and I saw so many people crying, but it was a soft beautiful cry. I didn't relate to these people anymore and I knew I couldn't say to them, "These are not my words, these are his." They didn't believe in that. I did know I had a special moment between he and I, and he came to tell me... I was right. Life does continue on.

My father's body was sent to UCLA. They wanted to study him to learn what made him live so long on dialysis. I remember Dr. A spoke at my dad's memorial—it stuck with me after all these years. A doctor understood that there is more to us than just flesh.

He said, "They are studying David at UCLA hoping to find the answers about him. They won't find the answers in his body—it was his spirit."

I agree.

Before I left Bob, I started to really listen to my intuition and make big changes toward freedom. The coffee shop I was working at when I left him wasn't doing so well—and I wasn't surprised. It was run more like a homey hangout than a real business. A young girl was managing it, and she pretty much gave the coffee away. Customers loved her, but because she gave out so much product and never tracked inventory, the place eventually went belly up. She'd charge people a dollar just to get bigger tips. Great for her pocket, but not for the owner's.

Before I moved to the Midwest, I had already decided to rise up at Starbucks and became a shift lead. I ran the floor, handled the money—it wasn't for the pay (just 75 cents more an hour), it was for the freedom.

So, with that shop gone, I was determined to make sure I wasn't out of a job. There was no way I was going to let Bob have any control over me again. I decided to apply to Barnes & Noble—I loved, *loved* books. When I was younger, I had dreams of being a writer. I never thought I was good enough... but hopefully, you'll like this book.

I heard they were opening a new Barnes & Noble, so I applied. I landed the job, and I was thrilled to finally be working in a bookstore—no slinging coffee, no scrubbing floors, just me and books. *Until* they found out I had worked at Starbucks for years.

They begged and begged me to work in the Starbucks café. I immediately said no! I swore I'd never work for them again. I used to have nightmares about working there—and honestly, I still do. The higher-ups from Barnes & Noble even came to meet with me and really tried to sell me on running the café. I told them I'd think about it.

And I did—I started thinking about the pay, the benefits, what a manager position could offer. After all, it *was* different than a regular Starbucks...

In the meantime, a friend of mine Katie told me of a new coffee shop opening. It sounded hip and cool—it was a startup company. I went there and it was basically a kiosk in a high-end version of Home Depot. They were opening an outdoor California-style mall. This was a small town and they were so excited about this new mall and even more excited for a Cheesecake Factory opening! Coming from L.A., I didn't get it—why everyone was so impressed. But this upscale, fancy version of Home Depot would house this new coffee kiosk.

I met the owner—he knew nothing about coffee!! It was called JAVA U and he was bringing it from Canada to the States. I started teaching him about how to clean the machines, how to make coffee—the interview turned into a class on coffee and equipment. He offered me the job on the spot. He said, "This company is going to grow and you can grow with it!"

This is when my intuition and my ability to see visions kicked in. Barnes wanted me, but Java U needed an answer that day. I looked at my future—I saw Barnes being stable, secure, something I knew, but also getting me more stuck. And I looked at Java U—they already had stores in New Jersey. I saw it as a ticket out of here! This was a startup company, no security—but in my gut, I knew.

I called Barnes that minute, told them I'd found a different job, and turned to my new boss and said, "I'm in!" That job ended up becoming so much more—I became the trainer for everyone who didn't know how to make coffee. I created the menu for the café I was working at. I taught him everything I knew, and in return, he taught me Excel, how to buy from wholesalers, how to track inventory. I even bought a briefcase. He gave me a salary. He sent me to Atlanta, where I trained new hires—they had stores out there, too!

I was turning into the very thing I'd avoided at Starbucks—corporate-like—but this time, it was saving me. I saw the irony: I had always resisted the corporate ladder, but now, the very knowledge I picked up at Starbucks was the thing setting me free. That was my first real lesson in how the future actually works. One decision leads to another and creates an outcome—not destiny, not pre-written fate. Just choices and results.

Eventually, I took over the entire kiosk. Every manager he hired before me failed—even my friend, the former manager of the other coffee shop. (Not that it was a huge surprise.) So now I was in charge of this failing kiosk **and** responsible for wholesale buying for all the East Coast stores, including Atlanta.

The important part? I was finally making enough to *save*. That's how I left Bob—I already had this job lined up. I started to come back to myself. I trusted my intuition again. After I finally left and moved into the attic, I was probably the happiest and most peaceful I'd been in years. I'd go to work for 14 hours, come home to my cats, grab my DVDs from Netflix (back when they came in the mail), watch them on my laptop, eat ice cream alone... and I was healing. I was happy.

I turned that kiosk into the number-one grossing location in the company. But I was ready for something new. I wanted to move to New York. My boss said, "If you can find a manager to replace you, and they can run the store successfully for at least a few months, then you can go." So that was my plan: interview, train, and test the right person. I ran the store like a machine.

We had a tiny storage space and I kept it fully stocked every day. I cut out the constant Costco runs and found local delivery for syrups and coffee from a small, amazing roaster. I arranged milk delivery through another store's vendor. I even ditched the crusty pre-packaged food and found a local catering company to deliver fresh sandwiches and pastries. Employees from the surrounding shops started coming to *us* instead of the Starbucks that had opened up—ironically, in the same mall.

We went from losing money to booming profits. So when it came time to find a manager to replace me, I was confident. I hadn't taken a break in months, so my plan was to train someone, take a few days off to test them, then eventually a full week.

I don't remember the other interviews—but one person stood out. He came in with a scraggly beard, long hair, totally unkempt. He looked like a wild hippie who'd just walked out of the woods. He said all the wrong things in the interview: told me he'd been fired from his last job for a dumb reason, said he'd been searching for work for a long time, and basically admitted he was desperate.

But I was using my intuition. I didn't need the perfect résumé—I needed loyalty. I needed someone who would *care* about this job, someone with nothing else distracting them. I could train someone like that.

As long as it wasn't someone who would start and quit in a few months, I was open. And I saw *all* of that in him. I knew—he just needed a break. So I hired him.

I didn't tell him to shave his beard. He had a wild forest on his face. So I said to myself, *"If he doesn't show up clean-shaven, then this won't work."* It wasn't about grooming—it was about commitment. It would be a sign to me that he was taking this seriously.

The next morning, he showed up: hair slicked back, face freshly shaven. He didn't drive, so his mom dropped him off—and yes, he was a full-grown-ass man. But when you've been through things in life—homelessness, loss, no money, no car—you learn to choose grace. You can either be understanding of people's situations, or you can become a Karen. I chose understanding.

I didn't care that he didn't drive. That had nothing to do with this job. I *got it.* I've mopped floors. I've struggled. I've been broke. I've had people die. That kind of life experience changes you.

I didn't grow up that way, though. I grew up in a big house—six bedrooms, a pool, two fireplaces, my own room, all the clothes a girl could want. We even had intercoms in the house. We were basically upper-middle class. But the path I chose—and the one I keep choosing—is the one *of the people.*

Is there a queen in me who loves spas and fine dining? Absolutely. But there's also the woman in me who sees people, loves people, even when they hurt or disappoint. Because I understand: shit happens.

I trained Jack. He had his moments—he could be stubborn, he pushed back sometimes. But, he always shifted. He always grew. He took the job seriously. I taught him customer service, how to hire, how to stock and prep. I had the files ready, the stockroom labeled, the paperwork organized and clear.

It was time.

I left him on his own for a few days. Then a week. Then I was only checking in once a week. I had other stores to deal with. I was traveling, training in Jersey and Atlanta. I had created the drink menu—one I won't share here because I'm saving it for my *own* coffee shop someday. (For now, it's virtual: The Medium Brew Café on my podcast. But one day, it won't be.)

Business was rolling. So, when I asked my boss if I could finally move to New York, he said yes.

I had saved money. I had a friend there who was going to help me. But in the end, I found the apartment myself—in Harlem. I was going to drive up. It was only an 8-hour drive. I checked it out to finalize things.

My potential roommate was pregnant. I didn't care—I love babies. And I think I might have been the only person she interviewed who *didn't* care. She told me she was unsure about me—a white girl moving into her place in Harlem. She said there weren't really any white girls in that neighborhood. This was 147th Street—not Apollo Harlem. That's where my other friend lived, off 125th and the A train. This area wasn't gentrified yet. I didn't care.

But my friend who I brought along? She was *shook.* She had never been in a Black person's home or a Black neighborhood in her life. And that shocked me. Especially because she *lived* in a city full of diversity—but it was still very segregated.

We walked up to the building. She looked nervous. We knocked—and the doorknob fell off. That, honestly, was more concerning to me than being in Harlem. I heard lots of voices inside. Then a woman showed up holding a baby.

I was confused. I *knew* she was pregnant, so... what was happening?

She laughed. "Oh, that's my nephew," she said, smiling.

She had on a durag and led me to the back of the living room where her family was visiting. We went into the kitchen, and we talked, settled things.

Later, she told me she knew she liked me because I didn't flinch at her family. She thought I would react to the number of Black people around me. I told her, "Nothing new for me." She knew my background, but she needed to see it for herself. She also said she was surprised I never asked about her durag. She laughed and said, "you passed the test." Then she cracked up again and added, "But, your friend sure did seem scared." I laughed and agreed.

After dropping off a few boxes at my friend's house, we headed home. I remember watching the *Sex and The City* finale with the woman I was renting from and her friends—it aired on February 22, 2004. That next week, I was moving to New York. All the women at the watch party were housewives, and they looked at me like I was about to embark on some grand adventure. You could feel their envy. They seemed bored, stuck in their big, beautiful homes, dreaming of a single life. I didn't envy them at all. I had one thing that mattered: freedom. And I had made it happen. I was going to New York to start a new life.

I drove across the country with my two cats—there was no way I was leaving them behind, and I couldn't afford a flight. Once I arrived and moved into my new place, two major things happened: First, I broke off my friendship with the only friend I had in New York. Once I got there, she didn't help at all—she said she was busy going out for drinks. In life, you really learn who your friends are when someone dies or when you're down, facing some of the hardest moments. She wasn't there when my mother was dying. Over the phone, she said she had her own problems. She wasn't there when my father passed, either. And now, during my divorce and this huge move? Same thing. She almost seemed to enjoy my struggle.

We'd had arguments like this before, and I had given her another chance. I believed we had grown past it. Eventually, she asked for forgiveness. And even though I did forgive her, it was clear—I still hadn't learned proper boundaries or self-worth. But I would.

New York, in the end, was incredible. My friend and I did eventually bond again, and I grew so much during my time there. I went through insane, unforgettable experiences. You know the phrase "a New York minute"? It's real. And I loved every one of them.

I left my job at Java U—it had been a great ride, but it was time. My roommate was awesome—super introverted. We lived in a T-shaped apartment: her room on one end, mine on the other. When I lost my job, she was worried I wouldn't be able to make rent. What she didn't know was—I'm a hustler. I got a job at another coffee shop and nannied during the day on the Upper West Side. (Not the East Side. If you know, you know.)

I was starting to wake up again. My intuition was growing stronger. But the city started to feel different. Harsher. I loved my friends there. My niece lived nearby—only 12 years younger than me—so we hung out a lot. But I could feel something pulling me home. When you're empathetic and compassionate, New York can be a lot to carry.

I dated around, kept it casual. I didn't want anything serious. I'd just spent seven years with a man—six of which were dry as a desert in the bedroom. I thought I'd wasted my good years.

Turned out, I didn't.

I healed myself in New York. And then, one day, I told the Universe:

Bring me someone artistic and grounded, someone who understands my spiritual side.

One week later, I got an email.

It was from my ex—Blake. The one with the awesome mom, Maxine.

I thought, *Whoa. He fits everything I asked for.*

My heart opened up again.

I emailed him back, gave him my number. He called.

And that one phone call? It shifted my entire world again.

Suddenly, my path was clear as day.

Chapter Nine
The Dead Speak

I called my ex, Blake, and we caught up. I told him I was living in New York now. I shared my saga with Bob, and he shared a little bit of what was going on with him. We always had a good friendship and gave each other a lot of support. He really helped me feel comfortable with my gifts—especially through his mother. She and I stayed in touch on and off, like Blake had asked me to. We always said that if we broke up, she and I would remain friends. That was important to him, especially since she had lost her daughter and didn't want to be hurt again after growing so close to me.

Eventually, I lost contact with her because of my relationship with Bob. I was too embarrassed. While Blake and I were catching up, his phone beeped and he asked me to hold while he checked the other line. I waited a while, and when he came back, he sounded down—distraught. He blurted out that he had just found out his friend had died.

I was dumbfounded and honestly a little freaked out. Why were we always connecting over death?! He explained that his friend had been sick for a while and that they knew his passing could happen at any moment. So it wasn't a surprise—but still. The timing was so strange.

I comforted him, but the whole thing was kind of surreal. Since he knew about my gifts, I wondered if he wanted me to try and connect to his friend. I asked if he wanted me to do that thing I used to do. He said yes without hesitation. I have to admit, it was nice to be my real self with someone again. That's what originally drew me to Blake—his full acceptance of this part of me.

He was never a huge believer, but he never made fun of me or his mom for it. So I tuned in.

When I do this, it's like a screen appears next to me. My abilities are very refined now, but they weren't back then. Before the vision comes, it always starts with feelings. I feel everything. It's like someone else's emotions suddenly take over. I'll feel sadness, happiness, annoyance—and it's confusing, because I know it's not me.

For example, I can be in a perfectly good mood and suddenly feel irritated for no reason. My tone might change—not my voice, just the energy behind it. My body language can shift. I might start using phrases I've never used before or mimic gestures. It's not conscious. I take on their emotions, their personality, the way they feel about the person I'm reading for. It could be love, regret, pride, frustration. That's how telepathy works—it's not words or logic. It's a knowing. A feeling.

The whole process feels like watching a movie. The tone sets first—like music playing before a scene begins. Then the imagery starts to pixelate, slowly becoming clearer. I usually look off to the right, where the "screen" comes into view. Then I start to hear—not audibly, but in my mind's eye—what the spirit wants to say. Visions, feelings, words, and symbols all come at once to form the message. It's fast—way faster than speech. And honestly, it feels more natural to me than talking ever has.

In that moment, reading for Blake, I felt like I *was* this guy. Kind of cocky. Kind of annoyed. Then I saw him—fuzzy at first, like he was still forming. He looked rough around the edges. And I heard him say he was pissed that he died. Said he'd rather be drinking and smoking and hanging out with "loose women." I repeated it to Blake and he immediately laughed, "Yup, that's him. He loved dive bars, cigs, and women!"

I was more shocked that I could still do it. My sight was a little rusty, a little glitchy, but I still nailed it.

Then I said, "He says he has a car he wants you to have."

Blake confirmed: "Yeah. He gave it to me before he died. It was too low to the ground, too fast. He wanted me to take it."

I smiled, still surprised at how much was coming through. I added, "He says thank you for everything. He's still not sure about this whole 'new realm' situation—but he'll get back to you on that."

That was all I could get in that moment. I was honestly shocked by how much came through so quickly, and how accurate it all was. We made plans to talk again, but when I hung up, I sat there just... processing.

Turns out, my gut had been pulling me home. Was it about Blake, or something else entirely? I wasn't sure, but I knew I needed to go back.

I had spent a year in New York, and I felt like I had gotten what I came for. I healed. I played. I had wild experiences, learned a lot, and had a good time.

But something was missing.

I felt... empty. Unfulfilled. Disconnected from myself. I wasn't living authentically. I had learned to talk to people and pretend I didn't *see* things. It was like watching someone walk around completely naked and pretending you didn't notice. Imagine the mental gymnastics that takes—everyone else sees them clothed, but you see what's underneath. That's what intuition is. Seeing what others don't. And pretending you don't.

I felt fake. Not grounded in who I was. I wore headphones on the subway and sunglasses even at night, just to block out the world. I tried to ignore how intense everything felt. Eventually, I realized I was afraid of turning cold. When I caught myself getting impatient with an elderly person taking too long to get off the train—thinking, "Move it, lady!"—I stopped and asked myself: Who am I? Who am I turning into?

This wasn't me. It wasn't who I wanted to be.

New Yorkers are some of my favorite people, but they pride themselves on being harsh and hardened. Say what you will about L.A., but we're mostly glorified hippies with a little splash of posh. At least the ones *from* here are. The ones who move here think it's all glam. But those of us born and raised—we're weird, intuitive, dreamy. We're La La Land for a reason.

I had spent so much of my life running—from home, from my past, from my true self.

It was time to stop running.

It was time to go home.

Chapter Ten
Gifts & Curses

When I got back to L.A. and saw Blake for the first time in person, it was pretty rocky. I had changed a lot since the last time I saw him. I was a different person physically, mentally, and spiritually. The last time I saw him was about eight years ago. I was younger, fifteen pounds lighter, and not as damaged. He had changed too. He wasn't the young, skinny, free-spirited rock star I used to know. He commented at one point on my looks—weight-wise (sigh)—which I thought was pretty bold, considering he was much bigger than me. I was 5'11 and now 140 pounds, and I wasn't in my twenties anymore.

I think this happens when you reunite with an old flame. It's hard to be in the present with them. You look at them with the eyes of the past. I started to question why I had come back to this relationship. In my heart, I wanted it to work so badly. He had been a good friend and the only person in my life who ever supported my true self. Sometimes you try to make that round peg fit into that square hole. Stepping back into relationships can always be risky, but I was back home and more in tune with my intuition than I had ever been before.

I was very focused and determined to rebuild my life in Los Angeles. I spoke out loud to the universe that I wanted to find a job in coffee. I also asked the universe to make transportation a non-issue. Blake had a car, but I didn't want to drive it. I was too nervous. What if I damaged it? The pressure was too much. I hadn't driven in a year, and I was rusty. Living in L.A. at that time—pre-Lyft and Uber days—not having a car made life extremely difficult.

Yes, I requested—that's how it works with the universe. You ask, not beg. Unlike religion, the universe expects you to know your value and claim what you want. We are taught not to demand what we need, but the universe is different. However, you must also give back. That energy exchange doesn't just mean money or volunteering once a year. It comes from who you are and usually unfolds naturally.

Maybe you're a lawyer who donates time to help friends or writes a legal blog. Then you tell the universe, "If I do this, bring me paid clients." The universe isn't a genie in a bottle—you have to meet it halfway. We are meant to live and thrive. Religion teaches we're lucky to get scraps, but manifestation is knowing what you want already exists in the ether. You're just pulling it into the physical.

I wasn't consciously aware I was doing this. It happened naturally. I was deeply aligned with the other realms. This might sound insane to the average person. Even I felt that way. But the other part of me knew something was going to happen.

The internet was improving. MySpace was a thing (don't we all miss MySpace?). Job hunting was easier. I was determined not to rely on anyone longer than necessary. Most of my life, I craved freedom.

I didn't exactly feel welcome in Blake's apartment. He had OCD and was very particular. The apartment had a decent-sized living room and kitchen, but it didn't feel like a place for a couple. The building had an outside pool and looked like something straight out of a typical L.A. movie—stucco walls, a single palm tree in the courtyard. Think *Singles*, and you'll get it.

I unpacked my suitcases but kept the boxes in the top closet. One day, I decided to pull them down to look for a blanket from my mother, Ruthie. She had crocheted it with blue and pink squares. In those days, you didn't know the baby's gender until birth. She kept the blanket in an old Wonder Bread bag, and I had carried it with me for years. I had planned to finish it for my own child someday.

The bread bag was thin, worn out. But when I looked for it, the blanket was gone. I tore everything apart and couldn't find it. I collapsed, sobbing. Years of grief hit me all at once. That blanket was the last piece of her I had.

I had shared a storage space with my ex-husband back in Seattle. Before I left New York, the owner told me I should stop paying—it was in Bob's name. Legally, they could only release my clothes and paperwork. The rest was either claimed or thrown away.

I had lost things in storage before—my modeling portfolio, old pictures. But this was different. This was my mother. A piece of her.

Growing up, my aunt wouldn't let me call her my mother. She wanted me to feel wanted by her family. She said, "I am your mother now, and this is your family." I know she meant well, but I had a right to claim the mother who gave birth to me. She didn't give me up.

I cried, but slowly I realized—my mother didn't live in that bread bag. I could feel her, hear her. I didn't need the blanket.

I once had a dream in my mid-twenties. It took me years to understand it—maybe fifteen. I dreamed I was walking along a path. A café table was outside with three women: one standing, two sitting with their backs to me. I stopped to talk to the standing woman. I sensed the two seated women were mother figures.

The one on the right reminded me of my grandmother—I could tell by the back of her neck. I couldn't see the woman on the left. The standing woman spoke strongly: "I am the only one you will speak to. They are not allowed. I will protect you. I am handling them for how they treated you."

I felt shame from the woman on the left. Submission from the one on the right. I woke up gasping for air. It felt like more than a dream. I didn't connect the dots at the time.

Years later, I understood. The woman standing was my mother, Ruthie. The woman on the left was my aunt. That's why there was shame. That's why I felt two mothers.

My mother was protecting me. She always had been.

She was speaking to me. The woman on my right in the dream was my grandmother. My grandmother didn't hurt me, but I suppose she witnessed things and didn't speak up. My mother Ruthie looked like a goddess, and it was clear she never stopped being my mother.

The blanket was just a mundane symbol of her—not her. I think that's why, to this day, I don't have much attachment to things.

I unpacked my clothes, but I kept everything else in my suitcases, always ready to go. I never fully made it my home. One day, while scouring the internet for work, I landed on an ad that made me stop in my tracks. It was for a mobile coffee and bar catering business—an idea I'd had years earlier. I got the job, and to top it off, the owner said he had no problem picking me up for gigs!

It felt like something out of the show *Party Down*. He handed me a white tuxedo shirt and tie, and I wore black pants. Catering gigs are huge in Los Angeles, especially for actors and musicians, because of the flexible hours. This job was a little different—we had to load and unload an actual espresso machine at every party we were hired for. Like the show, we were in a different environment each time. I loved that part.

When I got the job, Blake was shocked. He was amazed: "She said she'd get a job where she didn't need a car—and she did it!"

Around that same time, I began to go through a spiritual shift. I joined MySpace and stumbled across the psychic groups. I didn't know what I was doing—I just joined out of curiosity. I would sit and read through the chats where people were asking questions about their lives. I'd see the answers being given and feel this strong urge—"That's not right." I could feel it. I *knew* it.

I needed to help people. How could someone give such inaccurate answers? That kind of thing can really damage someone.

With my heart pounding and no faith that anyone would even care, I started answering people's questions. When I logged back in, I was shocked—there was a huge response. People were saying, "How did you know? This is completely accurate." I didn't expect that at all.

When I wrote, it felt like something was talking through me. I would tune in, focus on the person, and go into this space where the answers just flowed. Like artists describe when they're deep in creation. I answered more questions, and again, validation poured in. It kept growing. People started messaging me directly.

Even though I was excited and grateful, I still didn't know *why* this was happening, or what I was supposed to do with it. When you open gifts like this—when you stop denying them—the next question becomes: what now? What do I do with this?

And because I was still in the broom closet, I didn't know anyone else like me. The only people I had found were on MySpace—and they were the ones asking the questions, not giving the answer

I started practicing again with Blake's mom. Just knowing her and feeling her acceptance helped me so much. She belonged to a group for grieving mothers and was also a therapist. One day, she told me about a woman whose son had died and asked if I'd go with her to meet the mother—possibly to bring her some solace.

I told her I'd never really read for anyone in person besides her. Maxine said it was okay—we were just going to bring comfort. I agreed.

We made plans to meet at the woman's house. I arrived early, and Maxine called to say she was running late and to go in. I wanted to help Maxine because she had helped me so much.

As soon as I entered, I had a horrible feeling. The door closed behind me, and I thought, *Will I get out of here?* I didn't know why, but something felt dark.

The woman was nice enough but clearly broken inside. She invited me into her apartment. It looked okay, but I sensed she didn't leave her home much. She was excited to show me her son's room. I followed slowly, and as I rounded the corner, I saw a life-size doll lying on a bed. It looked handmade, fully clothed, with a photo taped over the doll's face.

She smiled at me and said, "This is my son's room. I kept everything exactly as it was before he died."

A chill went over me. I glanced at his computer—there was a printed photo taped over the dead screen. She said it stopped working, so she printed out an image of the screen.

Frantically, I thought, *Where the hell is Maxine?!* I understood this woman was in deep pain, trying to keep her son alive through objects. But, this was beyond my pay grade. I could tell she wasn't balanced, and I became afraid for myself.

Finally, Maxine arrived—looking completely unfazed. The woman showed her everything and said she wanted to celebrate her son's birthday. We sat down, but suddenly I saw roaches. Everywhere. Crawling across the couch.

I glared at Maxine. The energy felt dark—not just grief, but something denser. It was too much for me to read clearly. I couldn't.

The woman got up to get the cake. We followed her to the kitchen. More roaches. I whispered to Maxine, "I'm not eating this."

She whispered back, "Just wait. I know she's in pain."

Maxine understood her pain in a way I couldn't. I let her take the lead. I held the plate but didn't eat. Maxine did. We said goodbye and left.

That day, I learned something valuable: people focus on ghost hunting and act like it's just fun. But they forget—those spirits were someone's loved ones. Their pain and loss are real. It's not something to play around with. Ever. I never do. I ended up reading for that woman over the phone much later, when I had more experience. She was grateful and said it helped her.

At the time, my life was all about slinging coffee and logging into MySpace religiously. I was starting to change. Spirituality was becoming a bigger part of my life. Blake and I were doing okay, but he wasn't my focus. We weren't planning to get married. I supported his music and he let me explore my spiritual side.

The coffee catering job had its perks. One time, we booked a birthday party for Robert Downey Jr. I'd met hundreds of celebrities growing up in LA, but this was different. He was *'80s pop culture*—my teen years in one person.

We were hired just for him. Our coffee cart setup was impressive: a top-tier espresso machine with a copper dome cover and a little eagle emblem on top. The cart itself was industrial, but we covered it with black linen and topped it with marble tiles. Those tiles were beautiful—and heavy. Setup and teardown were no joke.

We used high-quality organic sugar cubes (brown and white), elegant stir sticks, and fancy napkins. Even the coffee mugs were plastic but designed to look like real glass. The whole setup looked sleek and high-end.

Behind the scenes, though, the owner was a mess—disorganized and frankly, kind of a creep. Once, when I suggested we update the uniforms, he smirked and said, "No, I hear all kinds of things about how people like you in that outfit."

Ew. I thought, *Okay, Hugh Hefner with a beer belly—I'm no Playboy Bunny, and your Sherman Oaks townhome is no Playboy Mansion.*

I just glared and said, "Well, they're outdated."

He stayed quiet, so I added, "Old-timey. Like something your grandpa would wear." Then I smirked and went back to setting up for Robert Downey Jr.'s party.

Our station was set up right by the front door. Once everything was good to go, my boss left—thank Goddess. It was just me running the bar.

Then Robert walked over. This was about a year before *Iron Man* came out—before the whole world realized he was about to rise again. He strolled up to the cart, and my stomach flipped. I'd met a lot of celebs before, but this was *Less Than Zero, Sixteen Candles*... RDJ was Gen X royalty.

He said, "I have that machine at home."

I smiled. "You do? This exact one? Are you sure?"

Okay, so I forgot this was Robert Downey Jr. for a minute. I was thinking, *This is a big and expensive espresso machine! People don't just have these in their homes.* Silly me—I forgot who I was talking to. He just brushed off what I said and replied, "Yup, I love it!"

He was the friendliest, coolest guy—the nicest celeb I've ever met. You know how they say, "Don't meet your heroes"? They're usually right. But this time, I was so glad I did. He asked, "Can you make me a four-shot cappuccino?" I said of course. Then he danced off like only Robert Downey Jr. can. I nearly died—oh my God, he's the coolest. He slid across the floor, swaying side to side in that classic, smooth way.

I pulled four shots of espresso, steamed the hell out of that milk, made the tightest foam, and walked over to him to hand him his drink. He was dancing on the dance floor—yes, *in his house*. He paused, took a sip, and said, "It's wonderful." He really had superhero energy.

I beamed and went back to my station. No one else cared about the coffee cart—there was a bar serving alcohol. But Robert was known for being sober, and coffee was his new thing. He now has a coffee company called Happy Coffee, and honestly, it fits him perfectly.

I didn't mind. I got to chill out by the front door and people-watch. It was the who's-who of celebrities. I've never really been starstruck—until that night.

I'm standing there, and I look up—and who do I see?

KEANU FUCKING REEVES walks in. He heads straight for my station.

Inside, I'm screaming like a teenage girl. Outside, I'm cool and calm—just another day. He was even more beautiful in person. He walks up and, in his Keanu voice, says, "Uh, can I have a cappuccino?"—like straight out of *Bill and Ted*. I'm very familiar with his voice—I've been playing *Cyberpunk* for the third time.

I look at him, thinking, *Can I speak? Can words even come out of my mouth?* Then all of a sudden, light bulbs start flashing behind him. I was kind of freaked out. I watched how he didn't flinch. For a brief moment, I felt for him. Imagine walking through life constantly being flashed and photographed—so often that you become immune.

He didn't even turn around. He just stayed present. That hit me. This isn't a normal way to live.

I barely managed to make the drink. I tried to pull myself together, but seriously—Robert Downey Jr. *and* Keanu?

I handed him the cappuccino. He picked up one of the big brown sugar cubes, dropped it in, took a stir stick, and wiggled it around, saying, "Th-ank y-ou."

I said, "You're welcome," and watched as he wandered off. He acted like he'd never seen a sugar cube before. Then he walked over to a wall where Sean Penn was sitting and just stood next to him.

Oh yeah—Sean Penn was there, just casually chilling. Then Sting walked in. Then Stephen King. And I had a front-row view.

There were some girls drinking and dancing, trying to get attention from the celebs. And, not your usual L.A. type with Botoxed and snatched faces—just regular, pretty girls. But Keanu stared straight ahead. I noticed how respectful he was. He didn't give off that ick vibe so many men do. He actually seemed kind of introverted.

Then someone walked in who had starred in *The Crow*. I wasn't a huge fan of his personally, but that movie? Easily one of my all-time favorites. He was chatting me up—not directly hitting on me, but it was clear what his intentions were. I was both flattered and slightly creeped out.

The irony? *The Crow* is all about the dead—about how they return to seek justice. It's about magick. And here I was, a baby witch and medium. A sign, maybe?

That night, I met:

- A guy from the unseen world (*The Matrix*),

- A superhero in the making (*Iron Man*),

- And a character that symbolizes the underworld (*The Crow*).

On the outside, I was just a coffee barista. But inside? I was awakening to my gifts—magick, mediumship, psychic ability.

My life was... a movie.

At the end of the party, I packed up. Robert came back over to chill with his wife on the couch. He said, "Thank you so much for doing this. It made my birthday special."

Wait—*he thanked me?*

I hadn't seen him since I made his drink earlier that night. I didn't think he even noticed. But yeah—I only made three drinks that night:

- Keanu Reeves (*Neo*)
- Robert Downey Jr. (*Iron Man*)
- Michael Wincott (*Top Dollar, The Crow*)

That's a sign if I've ever seen one.

I turned to Robert Downey Jr. and said, "Of course."

I'll never forget it. He reminded me we're all connected. If you take a moment to really *see* someone—no matter who they are—just be kind. Let people know they matter. It's not that hard. People have good days and bad days.

Remember:
"It can't rain all the time."

I didn't realize it then, but my origin story was being written in that moment. Something shifted in me. And after that night, I made a decision:

I was done running.
It was time to stop hiding and start accepting my true self.
I was going to become the best I could be.
I was going to hone these gifts.
It was time to come out—and face myself.

Chapter Eleven
The Ritual

The hardest part about having gifts like this is accepting that you have them. The second hardest is letting people know you do. I didn't share with anyone the journey I was on developing my gifts. My name started to circulate, and my MySpace page was gaining popularity. I wasn't MySpace famous, but the metaphysical world was different—smaller and more fringe. I was happy. I had a nice, small, consistent group.

I decided to create my own group page—think Patreon meets TikTok. I was excited I had built this following. I set up rules to protect people from trolls and made sure everyone felt safe, respected, and heard. People would ask me questions there, and I read them. My teachers were higher beings. I stayed away from learning from humans. Ego is such a problem in the spiritual world; I didn't want to be influenced.

I started to really bloom as a Medium. My focus was more on talking to those who passed than anything else, and the gratification of helping people was beyond measure. I didn't charge for readings. I practiced and honed my gifts the way a singer or painter would. If you were to ask me to choose my gifts, I'd rather be Adele than Adela. But I was learning to be okay with being Adela. I wanted to be the best I could so I could help people—not hurt them. Bad readers with ego really hurt people.

At some point, before I fully gave in to these abilities, I heard of a well-known Medium and bought his book. It mostly transcribed his readings and detailed his journey. His and Allison DuBois' books (the Medium the show *Medium* is based on) were the only ones I read. This Medium was holding a gallery event, and I decided to check him out. It was a huge crowd, and I sat in the audience hoping to be picked. You may have seen this on TV—the Medium gets up and then gets "drawn" to someone, giving them a brief reading.

I wasn't expecting much but secretly hoped he'd pick me. He mostly went on about John Edward, implying he was a fake. Then he told us he was supposed to have a TV show, but it didn't work out. I didn't know we were here to give this Medium therapy. It was odd and clear he was jealous. Then he did something even stranger: he asked everyone to stand up when he shouted the first initials of their deceased loved one. Then he'd add more details to see who stayed standing. It was Medium musical chairs. Is this Mediumship?

People in pain and grief become desperate. I was in pain, but not desperate. I also had the ability to hear and see the other side. He yelled out the letter F—my grandmother was Florence. Then he said the person had an accent—she had a New York accent. Then he said they were of European descent—my great-grandparents were Russian. It came down to me and another person. He looked at me, then them, and said, "You!"

I wasn't surprised. The person he picked looked so sad and desperate. I sat down and watched. He led them, prompted them—cold reading style. He read maybe three people out of over a hundred. Some Mediums use plants in the crowd, but I don't think he did. At the end, he pointed to a couple in the front row crying and asked, "Did you lose a child?" They stood up. He handed them a teddy bear and said, "They told me to bring this to you."

It all felt so theatrical and manipulative.

I went to another gallery a while later, more open this time. I looked around and said to myself, "If I have this gift, I will never do this to people. If I have a room full of people, I will read every single one."

He got up, did his thing. I hoped he'd pull my mother from his bag—he didn't. He was selling books, and if you bought one, he'd sign it. I figured the only way I'd know if he was real was if I looked him in the eye.

I bought the book, stood in line. Right before it was my turn, he handed another person a teddy bear and said, "Your loved one told me to give you this." Behind him was a whole bag of teddy bears.

My heart pounded. This man was hurting people.

He looked up at me and I glared into his steel blue eyes. He paused. I said, "Thank you," grabbed the book, threw it in the back of my car, and said, "Fuck that guy."

From that point on, I knew: I would have to learn another way.

I committed to my path. I just started reading people. I had a long list. I felt something say, "This is it. This is what you've been running from. Accept it. It's time."

One day, I lit four candles: one by my head, one by my feet, one on my left, and one on my right. This was all directed by that realm—they were telling me how to do this. I heard, "This is how you protect yourself—by creating a circle." It's not like I heard voices. It was more like thoughts, a knowing, a feeling.

I laid down on the bed in the dark, crying, and said, "Okay, what do you want from me?! I give up. I am tired of running from myself. Tell me what to do!"

I felt the impression of a woman and heard her say: "Imagine a gold light circling around your feet, then your ankles, shins, calves, waist, chest, face. You are protected in the gold light. Now feel yourself disconnect from the body. Fly up."

A vibration came over me, and I started to see an older woman—hair in a bun—like a strict teacher from back in the day. She said, "I am one of your first teachers, and you are going to learn from us. Human teachers and spiritualists tend to influence you, and you're too eager to follow. Humans have ego that gets in the way, so you will learn purely from us."

She told me, "One day you will read people in person. So start on the phone."

I felt loved, free, and surrounded by the most amazing sensation—like I was home. Somewhere familiar. She told me this was Home, where we all come from and return to. I could feel my body vibrating. I had never felt so free, so alive, so me.

I stayed in that state for about an hour. When I came back, I wasn't drained—I was energized. I had been told this was my initiation into the gift, and it was just the beginning of my true path.

After that, people started asking for readings on the phone. The first person who asked me, I was terrified to say yes, but I agreed. I did the journey meditation before each call: lit the candles, laid down, saw the teacher, and she said, "I will help bring you the spirits. You can't do it on your own yet."

She also told me to read in a chair and act as though the person was sitting across from me. I told her that was insane—I'd never read anyone in person. She laughed, "One day you will read so many people. Crowds of them."

No way. I could barely handle this phone call.

I read them in the dark with candles lit. It would take me an hour just to get ready. I'd read for at least two hours, and though it took me time to get the information, it came. People were passing my name around on MySpace. I'd go to my coffee job and read on my off time. I never felt like it was work. I loved it. It felt like a part of myself I'd denied for too long. I felt like me.

Still, I was far from knowing what I was doing—or where it was all leading. I hadn't told a soul except Blake and his mom. But I was giving away so much energy, and I started to notice that people were taking advantage—getting multiple readings every week.

Then I met a woman at a party—she was a hairdresser. For some reason, I told her what I did. She lit up. She was so encouraging. Maybe because I didn't know her, it felt safe—like I'd never see her again. But, she asked for my card. I told her I didn't have one. She asked, "Why aren't you charging?"

Charging? I thought she was nuts.

She said, "At least take donations. Honor your gift." She gave me her card and offered an exchange: a haircut for a reading. That seemed fair. I loved anything beauty-related, especially hair.

She told me to make business cards. She had her own salon, and she seemed so badass—so together compared to me. So, I listened.

I told her people might get mad. She said, "If they do, they aren't your people. The ones who are will support your work."

So I followed her advice. I told people: you don't have to, but donations are appreciated. And still, they kept taking advantage. So, I had to make it a requirement. And just like she said, the ones who didn't like it disappeared. The ones who appreciated it stayed.

I ordered some cards—cheap, horrible-looking ones—but it was a start. I used VistaPrint. The options were simple. They even misspelled my name. So I crossed it out with a pen and wrote it in myself. Bleak, but a beginning.

I was entering the next phase of my origin story. I was taking it seriously. Where was I going? No idea. But for the first time, things were clicking. I was starting to feel like me. I was finally getting comfortable in my own skin.

Something magical was happening. I had moved past the discovery phase into the apprentice stage.

There was no going back, and I was more than okay with that.

Chapter Twelve
The Bridge

If anything kept me in shape, it was the coffee catering job. It required a lot of heavy lifting. The owner asked me to manage the business—a promotion—and I even kept the van at my house. It was a white van with no windows, the kind that definitely looked like a criminal's van. I mean, I did manifest a car for myself... just a reminder: when you're manifesting, be specific.

I was grateful, and although I only used it for work, I was now picking up employees. I did exactly what I had done for Java U and revamped the entire setup. I organized everything and streamlined the system. My boss had some good points, but mostly he was a cocky prick and pretty misogynistic. He had a business partner I liked—an ex-Disney Imagineer who had designed the cart for the espresso machine. The machine sat on top of the cart in the van; when you pulled the handles, it eased right out. The wheels popped out, and underneath there was storage space for supplies.

I created shelving in the back of the van and secured syrups and coffee with bungee cords so nothing would slide. Before I took over, everything was just tossed in a pile, spilling everywhere. Eddie (the owner) used to wash milk pitchers and spoons in any bathroom sink he could find. This is how I learned that fancy-looking doesn't mean anything.

I brought in dish soap and a sponge and cleaned up the entire system. I treated the employees well. They told me, "I'll work for you, not him," because I got the load-in and load-out down to minutes. With him, it took an hour. With me, we could unload and set up in 30 minutes. I had to win his employees back because they had basically quit on him. I told them, "He won't be at the gigs." That sealed the deal.

At this point, I was managing events and spending the rest of my time practicing readings on anyone I could. I had started taking donations—I was grateful. It meant they respected the work I was doing. I started timing my readings and limiting them. I cut them down to an hour instead of two or more. I used to just let the clock run because I was obsessed with making everyone happy and being ethical.

I was building my speed and accuracy. It felt like I was making a difference. I noticed the reactions when I got something deeply accurate—a detail about someone's childhood or a trait of the spirit that matched exactly. It felt as though the spirit was sitting next to me, telling me things, and I was passing it on to their loved one. I didn't hear them audibly—it all came through my mind's eye. Visions started to come faster. It was like combining different languages: visions, knowing, feelings—all at once. That's how telepathic communication works.

The hardest part was trusting what I saw or felt.

I had a client I read for many times. Her friend had died suddenly in a car accident, and she was secretly in love with him. He became a teacher for me—just like Blake's sister had been. Blake's sister showed me so many things, like how the spirit realm worked. I trusted her because I had so much validation from her mom.

Once, Blake's sister came to me in a dream. I was in a canoe with my father. He was rowing and told me he was taking me across the water to another land. When we got there, I got off the boat. I asked him if he'd be okay getting back. He said yes, and I told him goodbye. As I stood there, Blake's sister greeted me, and suddenly something inside me released. I could see her just as clearly as I see this computer screen.

I said to her, "I can see you so clearly now. This isn't a dream. I know I'm somewhere else."

She said, "Yes, it's true."

I asked, "Why can't it be like this all the time?"

She ignored me and said, "Focus, I want to show you something. Look at this man." It looked like he was coming out of a portal. She asked, "What do you see?"

I described the man. She said, "No, read past what you see." I saw his spirit—a darker, troubled being. She said, "Correct," and with a snap, I was back in the dreamy state, then I woke up.

What people don't understand is why they don't see spirits or that realm. The veil isn't something external—it's you. The veil is over your own eyes, created by fear and non-belief. That's why it doesn't "thin" in October. Your willingness to see that realm is what thins it.

The next time I read that client, her spirit friend said, "I'm going to show you how to see in her house." I didn't understand. He said, "It's like you're seeing across time and space."

He took me through her house. I saw patches of color on the walls. I told her what I saw. She said, "Oh my God, yes—I'm trying to paint. Those are samples."

He took me into her closet. I saw new red undergarments. She laughed, "Yes."

Remote viewing isn't like astral projection. My spirit doesn't leave. It feels like I'm a drone flying across the planet. I'm both the screen and the controller. I walk through their house, see the layout, the walls, or even past and future conversations. I only use this with permission or if I'm worried about someone. It feels like I'm holding a remote control with a screen.

Think of Eleven from *Stranger Things*. That gift? Remote viewing.

It was like I was the messenger between two people who could have had love, but one died too soon. That client was always respectful of my time. She and her mom once sent me a necklace they had in their family. I still remember the notes and little gifts I got in the mail. They meant everything. They validated that what I was doing mattered.

And for the first time, I believed that maybe... I mattered too.

Most things in life I could learn, but it came with tremendous effort. Things tend not to line up for me. Things tend not to click, and in general life came difficult. But this—this flowed so easily I wasn't used to it. And, although it may seem obvious now, I didn't realize then that it was because this was a gift.

I didn't chase it—I gave into it. I did feel myself changing. My abilities were growing and becoming stronger, and I allowed myself to accept this. It started to happen even when I wasn't reading. I started to see and hear things walking around. I was trying to control it. When I was around people in public, I would see spirits around them. I had a hard time blocking it out. Eventually, I learned how to control it and to purposefully see only what was in my mind's eye. I never walked up to them, but I could see if they'd lost someone—and who. I also started to learn I needed to protect myself and turn the volume down.

One of my employees needed me to drive him home to Pasadena. I was happy to. I knew what it was like not to have a car, to struggle. Struggling has been part of my life, and I felt so lucky to have this job. We were driving home over a bridge, and I kept seeing in my mind's eye images of people jumping off. It looked like they were taking their own lives.

Without thinking, I turned to him and said, "Why are people jumping off this bridge?"

He turned to me sharply and said, "What did you just say?!"

I had forgotten myself for a minute. I repeated it: "I see people jumping off this bridge."

He stared at me. "Adela, do you know about this bridge?"

I shook my head. "No."

"They call this 'Suicide Bridge,'" he said. He explained something about the stock market crash and how it led to a lot of suicides there.

I had no idea. Of course, this opened up the conversation for him to ask how I knew, and why I was seeing this. I told him, "Okay, I'll tell you. But you can't tell anyone."

He promised. So I told him about how I see things, how I'm a medium, and about my journey—how I'm learning and practicing.

He paused. "Oh my God! My friend and I—we love this sort of stuff. She's my roommate. YOU HAVE TO MEET HER!"

I was mortified. "You can tell her, sure, but no one else, okay?"

He agreed. We arrived at his place, and he invited me in. Knowing me, I probably had to pee—I don't remember. We went in and his roommate was there.

He immediately blurted out, "OH MY GOD, SHE'S A PSYCHIC AND A MEDIUM!"

I nearly melted into the floor. I knew he'd tell her—but not in front of me! I froze.

She turned to me, beaming. "Really?! I LOVE THIS STUFF! I WANT A READING!"

She was so friendly, bubbly, welcoming. I was exposed. There was no more hiding. It was the first time I told anyone outside of MySpace, and the first time I stood in broad daylight, exposed like a daywalker.

I told her sure—mostly because I felt this need to stop hiding. I figured, well, it's just the three of us. Why not?

At this point, I had graduated from donations; it had been almost a year. I had moved to charging a small amount. We set up the reading—over the phone, I thought. But I came to her house. It was a huge deal to me. I was so nervous. I really didn't know how this would go. I sat down with my journal. At that time, I used journals to scribble down whatever I saw. It helped me track it.

Back then, I didn't know how to control the spirits. I would let whomever wanted to come in, come in. So I talked to several people from her family. That's also why it used to take so long. I kept going until the person they wanted came through.

One spirit came through, so sad. He said he loved her. She started to cry. I felt this dark cloud with him. I asked him telepathically, why does your energy feel so sad? Why are you apologizing?

He said he did this to himself. He made me feel like I was in pain. In readings, spirits will take me through what happened to them when they died. I feel everything. Usually, they don't overwhelm me. He wasn't trying to—but he wanted it to be clear.

So I said to her, "Did he take his life?"

She said yes. Her voice cracked. "That's my boyfriend. He committed suicide."

You'd think I would have put two and two together—the bridge that led me to her. She was my first real, in-person reading. I'll be honest—I didn't put it together until writing this, twenty-four years later.

She cried. I kept going. Finally we came to the end, and then I asked her if I could intuitively read her. Blake once had a reading from a famous medium his mom took him to. He didn't want to go, but he wanted to support her. The medium gave him a psychic reading, but it was horrible and way off.

I felt I could do better. I was getting things from her already. So I tried. I was so nervous she'd say no—but she loved it.

Here's the thing I've learned from reading for many years: everyone loves hearing about themselves. Everyone wants to know something about themselves. People will most likely say yes—but you have to ask their permission first.

So, with her permission, I read her. I nailed everything. I kept getting scared she'd get upset. In the past, when I told people about themselves, they'd get mad. But, it resonated with her.

I was evolving. I was learning. If you ask permission and it's in a formal setting and you act professionally—it changes everything. My sight flowed. It felt so right, like I finally allowed myself to bloom.

I finished — I was elated. I had never read in person before. Wow.

I decided I'd wait and see if I was really ready to read people in person now.

I didn't wait long. Because what I didn't know about this girl—Layla—was that she knew everyone. She was the biggest social butterfly! She told everyone. I mean, she shouted it from the rooftops.

My phone started ringing. All her friends started asking for readings. Not only was I pushed out of the broom closet—I was shoved.

One of her friends called and said, "I want a reading, please."

I asked if she meant talking to someone who passed.

"No, no," she said. "The other thing."

I was shocked. She meant the psychic-type reading. That wasn't what I was used to doing. The only time I had done it was with Layla.

I asked if she was sure.

"Yes, please."

The day of her appointment, I arrived at her house. She was very friendly and welcoming. Her mom was there, but we went into another room. She was nervous her mom would hear us. I told her no problem—I understood.

So I let myself focus. I dropped in.

My system at this point was to do a meditation journey before the reading. The teachers would show me all I needed to know. I would write down anything I saw in my journal before I met them. It took me an hour of going through the journey.

I was so nervous. I started to tell her things I saw—about her, who she was, what her childhood was like. I looked and saw her future. She wrote it all down. Some she understood, some she didn't—but she trusted me.

She seemed younger than me. At that time she was in her twenties.

I was in my thirties, she took it all in. She cried and thanked me. I was probably with her for almost two hours. I felt so good—to help people.

I still know her, and years later she told me, "You know the stuff you told me? I wrote it down. At the time, I didn't understand it. I pulled it out one day and re-read it, and all the things you said came true."

Back then, I didn't know how to see timelines as clearly—I was still a baby reader. Not like I can now. But the validation, even years later, was so beautiful. I loved that she took the time to tell me.

Layla passed my name around to so many people, I called her and laughed, "How the hell do you know so many people?" She laughed back and said, "I know! I'm telling everyone!"

Word of mouth is your best friend in this work. Because it's so intimate, and there are so many scammers, people trust a friend's recommendation way more. I was grateful—but also felt something telling me it was time to go to the next level.

My professor—the old crone I worked with from the other realm—told me in one of my journey meditations that she was done teaching me. I didn't understand. "What do you mean you're done?"

She told me it was time to move on to the next teacher. I had learned from her how to listen to guides. She once told me I would read in front of crowds. I couldn't imagine it. She instructed me, "When you read people on the phone, in the dark surrounded by candles, imagine the person sitting across from you."

I did as she said. But I couldn't imagine leaving that safe bubble with my guides. Now it was happening. My name was being passed around in real life.

One of my first in-person readings was with a woman who had lost her adult son to suicide. I'd read for her several times for free back in my "training" days. She came to Los Angeles and wanted to meet in person. Since I didn't have a space, we met somewhere neutral.

After the reading, she told me how much I helped her and handed me a card. I didn't open it until after she left—I didn't want to break the energy. When I did, there was a kind note and a donation. She wrote that I deserved it, that I saved her and helped her heal.

I started to feel the weight of my abilities—the impact they could have on people's lives. I was so thankful, to make a impact. This was no longer just something I did on the side. My name was spreading, and I wasn't advertising—it was all word of mouth.

I don't like cold advertisement. I want people to understand how I work. My connection to that realm was growing. I believed I was connected to guides and energies, but my logical side still needed confirmation. Confirmation helps you trust what's happening.

I started doing more in-person readings, but I was still nervous. For one appointment, I asked for a bird as a sign that spirit was with me. I used to see birds all the time—they'd come to me naturally. My teachers warned against asking for signs on demand, but this time I needed it.

No birds showed up. I was disappointed, but I walked into her apartment trusting the process. As soon as I entered, a bird flew across the room. I thought I was hallucinating.

She laughed and said, "Oh, sorry—that's my pet bird. I let her fly around the house. Are you okay?"

Signs don't usually work on demand, but I was still learning. The spirit world prefers to surprise you when you least expect it, so your mind won't overanalyze it. I didn't tell her about the sign—it was more special that way. I keep a lot of what I see to myself. It's like I'm moving through the unseen world even while grocery shopping.

If you have magic happen to you, keep it to yourself sometimes. Magic gets lost in translation.

I told her no problem and proceeded with the reading. I was learning to navigate my sessions better. After each journey, I'd focus on the person and see a guide say, "I'll tell you all about them." I'd write it down before the reading. I felt pressure to prove it was real. I didn't want people to think I Googled them. So I focused on tiny details—conversations they had the night before, dreams they never told anyone. That built trust.

People always ask me: Can anyone learn how to read? I say you can teach someone to play piano, but not everyone becomes a concert pianist. I do believe people have gifts, but many are scared to show their true selves.

That's why I'm writing this book. It's why I record a podcast and why I post videos.

My "powers" were growing. But there was a downside. People looked at me differently. I saw the world differently. Unmasking people comes with a price. This work is a lonely path—you do it because it's who you are. Any reader worth their salt runs from it before they finally give in.

I was thankful for Layla and all the people she brought me. I started feeling a push to find a place to read—to quit the coffee job and go full-time. It had been a year of pure practice, and I felt ready. But, I was terrified. Who was I to say I could be a full-time reader?

Layla pushed me so hard. She lit up my world. Around five years later, she passed—very young—from a rare heart condition. I won't tell her story; it's not mine to tell. But she didn't know she was my first real reading. She pushed me so far out into the world and shined her light on me.

She still shows up. She's gotten me through rough times. It was the first time, but not the last, that my worlds collided. Besides my parents, she was the first person I connected with on the other side who I had known here.

I don't believe everything happens for a reason. I believe we create reason. Our decisions ripple outward. If you listen to that voice inside, to that knowing, it not only connects you to the other realms—it connects you to yourself. It allows you to live in your true skin.

It was time for me to fully come out and stop hiding. I thank the spirits who guided me. I thank those like Layla who lit the path.

And it would take reading in the park—with ants crawling over me and human pee in the grass—to finally push me out into the world.

Chapter Thirteen
The Pirate Witch Store

     I was introduced to the concept of raising vibrations by my teachers through my daily meditative journeys. Today it's a popular expression. People now say things like "good vibes," "high vibes," or "let's raise our vibration." I even see it on T-shirts. Back then, I used to say, "You need to raise your vibration to connect to the other realm," or I'd explain how I could feel people's energy even when we weren't in the same room. I would use technology metaphors—"It's like Wi-Fi"—to help people understand how I connected. As tech advanced, it became easier to explain the realm. I see it as a science we just haven't caught up to yet. At first, people didn't understand, but slowly they started to.

I loved the ritual—still do. My process: I lay down, light candles to form a protective circle, and begin feeling the energy build from my toes to the top of my head. I visualize a ring of gold light wrapping around each part of me, rising faster and faster. I use music to connect, letting the rhythm spin my energy into a cyclone. This helps me access the other realms. I practiced every day for an hour. Now I teach this in my classes to help others return to their spiritual home, and people often cry from the familiarity—a homesickness for a place they forgot.

Raising your vibration isn't about being better than anyone. Our energy here is dense and slow. The other realms are fast, light, unburdened by time or space. When I re-watched *Contact*, the part where Jodie Foster's character is encased in a spinning sphere, I got it. That spinning energy—that vibrational shift—that's what this is. I'm not saying I left my body physically, but raising vibration works in a similar way.

One time, after asking to see the beings I sensed, I lay down as usual and heard, "Are you sure you want to see us?" I said yes. Immediately, my body froze. I thought I was having a stroke. I saw myself crawling on the floor while my physical body was stuck on the couch. I now know that was my spirit body. I tried to yell for Blake but couldn't. Two beings in black cloaks appeared. They said, "Get up! Just get up!" like I was a toddler afraid to walk. I crawled to Blake, who was napping. He rolled over and pulled the covers up like he sensed me. I snapped back to my body and bolted upright, gasping.

This was familiar—I'd had sleep paralysis all my life. It's what happens when the spirit tries to leave but gets stuck. Later, it happened again, but I got up that time. Afterward, I asked Blake if he heard me. He said he didn't, but heard someone say, "Don't help her. She has to learn."

What?!

He wasn't even a full believer, which made it even more validating. I wasn't ready to meet them then, and they knew it.

It wasn't the first time something strange happened with Blake. When we were together the first time in my twenties, I had a dream where I was sitting at a metal table. Beings in white coats moved around the room. A child-sized being with almond-shaped eyes (not gray alien style, more human-like) sat across from me. I said, "So they know about you? You exist?" He said yes. Then he said, "I'm going to explain all the secrets of the universe, but you won't remember. They'll unlock when needed."

I looked at his mouth and said, "You don't have one."

"Correct."

Then it hit me—a flood of information—and I woke up. I asked Blake, "Did I leave?" He hadn't heard or seen anything. At that time, I wasn't even into aliens.

Blake was cool like that. He introduced me to *Coast to Coast AM* with Art Bell. We listened on late-night drives. It was eerie, weird, real. People called in with stories about ghosts and aliens. Art was open-minded and nonjudgmental. He was an inspiration for my podcast *The House Medium*, where people send in their stories, and I use my sight to help interpret what happened. Art died before I ever got to be on his show. That dream died with him. The new host just isn't the same.

Another time, Blake and I saw a black triangle-shaped craft hovering over Ventura Blvd in daylight—silent. We both saw it. As we exited the freeway to snap a picture, it vanished.

Years later, I met a retired Air Force captain in the strangest way. I was leaving a paranormal convention in Utah and had scheduled a Lyft to the airport for 4:30 a.m. It got canceled last minute. I panicked. Then—ping! A new driver accepted. He arrived in a clean car with a garment bag hanging by my seat. Odd.

"You headed somewhere?" I asked, nodding to the garment bag.

"Oh, that's my uniform. I work airport security."

"TSA?"

"No, I work in the towers."

Still not getting it.

"I watch for unusual things."

"Like passengers? Trouble?"

He chuckled. "No. I look for unusual things *in the sky*."

Wait, *what?!*

He casually shared he was a retired Air Force captain. He said, "We make those triangle crafts. They're man-made. But I've seen others—I've even sat in them."

He said it like he was telling me about his favorite sandwich. Calm. Casual.

Then he asked me what I did. I figured, screw it. I told him I was a intuitive, a medium, and I remote viewed.

He nodded, "I know what that is. What's your process?"

I told him. He listened without interrupting. Then he said, "I'm surprised the government hasn't approached you."

Excuse me, *what now?*

I was curious where this was going, so I said, "I'd be open to that.

He dropped that and changed the subject.

We got to the airport. He popped the trunk, handed me my suitcase, smiled, and said, "Great talking to you I could pick your brain all day. Enjoy your flight."

And that was that.

People have speculated maybe it was a test. Maybe the government was watching. I don't know. But something about that man, that ride, stuck with me. He said so much— without saying anything at all.

If anyone reading this has insight into that... I'm listening.

Once, while getting ready for a medium reading over the phone, I did my usual tuning in beforehand. I had the door open to the bedroom and saw someone walk by wearing white tennis shoes. I said something to who I thought was my boyfriend, but got no answer. I got up—and there he was on the couch watching TV. I asked, "Did you go to the bathroom?" He said, "No."

I closed the door to do the reading and started describing a man with white tennis shoes. I was shocked when the client said, "Yes, that's my friend—he was a huge sneakerhead."

After that reading, I made rules with the spirits. I was starting to learn you have to make rules. My first rule was: no appearing in front of me. I also said no touching, no talking to me out loud, and no disembodied voices!

I'm not so strict about the touching today. I just get poked sometimes, which is okay. I'm open to seeing them in front of me now, but for the most part, I don't. It's very jarring, so I stick to seeing with my mind's eye.

It's hard to explain what it feels like being a medium. You feel what the spirit feels, you see it through their eyes—like them. So boundaries are important. I was working on them then. I'm a pro now.

One area I can't fully control is while I sleep. I hate sleeping. I know all you sleepers don't get this—those of you who cuddle in bed and love the idea of sleep. Not me. It's a battle. I have to trick myself to sleep. I usually start on the couch first and fall asleep around 10 p.m. I wake around 1 a.m., then go up to bed and if I'm lucky wake again at 5 a.m. My whole life, I've woken up around 3 a.m.

There's no magical reason for that time—it's because we dream right before we wake, and spirits can meet us in that state. So I trick them. I'm still working on it. Nighttime is just something to get through, and because I'm such a morning person, staying awake at night isn't an option.

So even though I was growing, learning, getting faster, and having amazing experiences—I was still afraid to fully dive all the way in.

A woman contacted me for a reading—someone referred her to me. She wanted it in person. I didn't have a location to read in, so I suggested the park. She was okay with it, and I thought to myself, "Okay, so I don't need a spot. I can meet people at parks, beaches, etc. It'll be easy."

We set a time and day to meet. I sat under a tree—then bugs and ants came. I didn't think to bring a blanket. We moved, and a man walked by and said, "Be careful, the homeless pee here."

Great! This didn't make me look good. I looked so unprofessional. But, then again I wasn't really a pro yet. Luckily, I did a wonderful job on her reading.

After that, I knew the universe was saying: Get going. It's time to find a spot.

I didn't have a car, so I was walking a lot and I saw a place nearby had opened up. It was a witchy store—with pirates in front. It smelled like incense. They sold tarot cards, renaissance and pirate clothes. It was witch meets pirate store.

I was going to ask if they had readers and if I could read there. They'd just opened, so I thought it was perfect. My heart was pounding—I wanted to run—but I knew it was time.

I walked up to the lady at the front and asked. She said, "Well, the owner is here." I met her—she was so friendly, so witchy looking—I immediately loved everything about that place. I felt more like me than I had my whole life. The smell, the weirdness—it was like I ran away with the circus.

Witchy and paranormal movies like Harry Potter and Wicked are popular. Shows like Charmed—people love them. But in real life, people don't like real witches, psychics, or healers. We're still the weird ones to the masses.

I told her I was a new reader looking to read. She was receptive and had no problem with me doing readings there! She said she didn't have a spot in the store, but she did outside and could put a curtain up. The backyard was huge—looked like a magic garden without the garden. I loved the idea. L.A. weather is always nice, and the spot was covered.

I told her I had another job but could do both—let's just see. I'd found my home. I couldn't believe it was walking distance from my house. Again—everything was clicking. Everything was moving into place.

They said they wouldn't take a percentage of my readings—yet. Most places take 30–50%. I didn't know that then, so the fact they just wanted to have a reader and let me build clients was so generous. I only offered hour readings—I didn't know how to do short ones yet. It felt more professional. I had a place to read!

I was still working my coffee gig, but my boss was treating me more and more like shit. Again, I felt the tides pushing me toward a new direction—but I wasn't ready yet.

We had a gig. A wedding. It must've been over 100 degrees in the middle of August in the Valley. I was to do this gig alone. For some reason, he had no help—maybe trying to save money. He was getting greedier, forgetting I was the reason he could take vacations and breaks, and not have to attend gigs.

He used to make me wait to get paid. I had to pull up to his house, sit in my car until he told me to come up. One day, he called me over with his partner—the Disney guy—and they both laid into me about everything I was doing wrong, down to how I folded tablecloths. It felt like my acting teacher all over again.

I sat there simmering. When I get really mad or scared, I get quiet—not loud. I wasn't scared. I was furious. This has been a theme in my life—especially with men. If they saw I was forward, smart, efficient, successful—more than them—they always tried to "tame" me.

I let them go on. At one point they said, "If you can't learn these things, we might have to let you go."

I paused, reading them faster than they could talk. I took a deep breath and said, "Oh, okay. If this isn't working out, I should for sure leave."

My boss quickly retracted. The Disney guy followed his lead. They apologized, said, "I'm sure we can figure this out." Blah blah.

I knew they were trying to control me, shrink me, and not let me know my value. I read both of them. This problem wasn't going away.

So the day of the hot wedding—I thought I was going to pass out. He kept pushing me. I kept saying, "I can't do this. I'm going to pass out." He yelled at me. This fucking weak man.

I almost left that very moment. But, I looked over at the bride. Just married. Happy. Excited about her wedding. I just couldn't ruin her day because this man was an asshole.

I already had my mind made up—I was going to quit. Just not today.

I set up with him. He of course, left and went somewhere cool while I worked. He came back, we broke down, loaded the van. I said nothing. Calm and cool.

Right before I got in the van, I had a plan to make him wonder, to sweat it out. To mind-fuck him—all those days he made me wait to get paid, made sexist jokes, under-appreciated me.

I turned to him and said, "Oh, by the way, Monday we should talk."

He laughed nervously. "Can you just talk now?"

I said, "No, I don't think so. I think it's better Monday."

He said, "Are you quitting?"

I just laughed. "We should really talk later. I'm hot and tired. I better go."

I got in the van—windows down, because of course this piece of shit wouldn't fix the conditioning. I smiled all the way home. I felt better than I had in a year. I felt as though that van was driving itself.

I knew my life was about to change—and I was the one choosing it.

Remember, I don't believe everything happens for a reason. I believe the future forms from whatever decisions we make. Each decision affects the next and determines the outcome.

I had just created my future. And, I knew he was sweating.

Never, ever let anyone hold anything above your head!

Chapter Fourteen
The Seer

      I decided to read full-time around 2006. This was still pre-social media, and YouTube was just starting to become a thing. Phones weren't like they are now, and filming equipment felt complicated and expensive. I continued to connect with people on MySpace—it was still a great platform. Many people I met there, I still know today.

The pirate store was an awesome place to read, and I decided I was going all in. My relationship wasn't going well (surprise: the relationship that didn't work in our twenties also didn't work in our thirties). He wasn't thrilled about me quitting my job and already felt pressure to take care of us, even though he didn't fully support me. I kept my bags and boxes in his closet. I was always ready to leave.

I almost did. When I first moved back from New York, I had a feeling it wouldn't work out. I called my Aunt B and told her I was leaving. She said, "Adela, you keep running. You have to stop at some point and settle in. You can't keep running from yourself." Aunt B was my dad's sister, in her eighties then. Wise and calm. She grew up in the Seventh Day Adventist Church—religious, but never judgmental. She has always been my biggest cheerleader. Even now, we talk two to three times a week. She's really all I have left that feels like a parental figure. When she told me to stop running, I listened. I stayed. And I'm glad I did—because I found myself.

Monday came. I was meeting with my boss, and nothing was going to stop me. I felt it in my bones: it was time to quit. I wasn't just going to walk away; I wanted to do the right thing. I gave two weeks' notice to get things in order.

His business partner, the Disney guy, told me about a server I could use to build a website. That may not seem like much today, but in 2006, websites were expensive—thousands of dollars. No Wix . It was pretty innovative. I was ecstatic. It gave me a space to build something real. My bare-bones site: Adela, Intuitive & Medium.

At that time, I didn't even know what to call myself. But I printed business cards—this time, they spelled my name correctly. I added a symbol from a dream. My dad was in the sky, clouds floating around him. He showed me a staff with two vines intertwined, glowing cobalt blue with wings. He said, "Your gifts come from here. From home—where we come from, and where we return."

That image meant everything. The staff was me, walking the path. The two vines were the parts of me—my intuitive side and my medium side. The wings were a reminder that my gifts came from beyond this world.

I chose to use the titles "Intuitive" and "Medium." I wanted it to be clear these were two separate readings. I didn't call myself a psychic because of the stereotypes. Back then, no one really knew what an "intuitive" was. I had to explain: intuition is how I feel people, see outcomes, understand timelines, and remote view.

I do a lot of things differently. I don't use the word *psychic*— I prefer *intuitive*. I don't believe in reincarnation, and I'm not really into the moon or its phases. I like the idea, sure, but for me, it's always been more about the sun.

Being spiritual has to resonate with *who you are*—not what's trending or what others expect. It has to feel real. Authentic. Aligned.

Mediumship was more familiar because of shows like *The Medium*, Sylvia Browne, and John Edward. Still, my way of reading was different. I could talk to any spirit someone asked for—no backstory, no name needed. I wanted to spend the whole session connecting them to someone they loved. It wasn't about guessing; it was visiting.

Today, many people use "psychic medium" as a catchall. I don't love that. I believe intuitive and medium are different abilities. It's like the Marvel universe. Each hero has a specific power. That's how I see the psychic world.

I started reading at the pirate witch store, working the front counter to meet people. It wasn't how I imagined it would start, but I embraced it. I met renaissance folks, pirate cosplayers, and Disney creatives. When customers asked me for help picking out gifts, I tuned in to their energy. I'd say, "This ring feels more like them," and they'd ask, "How did you know?" That gave me the perfect opportunity to tell them what I really did. It was fun, magical, and felt like I had finally found my tribe.

Readings poured in. I was going over an hour because I didn't know how to set time boundaries yet. My process was to meditate on someone before they arrived, write what I saw, and use that during their session. With mediumship, I always reached who they needed—boyfriends, aunts, grandmothers, even old friends. I was starting to really *see*.

Then came the turning point: I realized the guides I was seeing were actually the spirit of the person. One day, I meditated on a new client and saw a guide. When she walked in, she looked exactly like the vision. I panicked, confused. I reached out to spirit and was told, "You are now one with us. You don't need intermediaries. Just tell them what you see."

It was terrifying. I called my hairdresser friend who had supported me early on and asked if I could practice on her. She agreed. I told her I wouldn't be using guides anymore. I would read from pure connection. And it worked. It flowed. I wasn't channeling—I *was* the connection.

That's when I knew: I was stepping into my role. I was a Seer.

A few years earlier, I had a dream of my mom. She was standing in her white nightgown, next to a glowing threshold. It looked like the gates of Disneyland. She said, "You can't go this far." I begged. I didn't want to leave. Then she showed me a massive line of people behind a rope. "They need you," she said.

I didn't understand that dream until much later. Until I began to read full-time. Until strangers wept in front of me, thanking me. Until I stopped hiding. Until I put my real name on my site: Adela Lavine.

Lavine was my mother Ruthie's last name when she died. She kept her second husband's name. I never got to use it growing up, but I took it back. "Adela" came from the Legend of Las Adelitas, the women soldiers of the Mexican Revolution. My mother named me to give me strength. And now I knew why.

There's a picture of her pregnant with me. She's in a blue sundress, facing the camera, glowing. Her sister—my aunt—stands behind her, facing forward. That picture always whispered to me: "I am your mother. I love you. I won't be here to raise you, but she will. And we both love you in our own ways. Be strong. Be brave. I wanted you."

Now I walk with my staff. With my sight. I have chosen to see. I honor my gifts. I hone them. And, I help people every day to connect, to heal, and to remember.

When I go home one day, I'll see my spirit family. They'll say, "You did good. We were always with you."

I was never truly alone.

Follow yourself. Follow no one. Listen to your inner voice.

Thank you for reading. See you soon.

Acknowledgments

To my clients — you've let me into your hearts and allowed me to walk with you through the most vulnerable moments of your lives. You trusted me with your loved ones and allowed me to be a guide. You often tell me I've helped you, but truly, you've helped me. I am honored and privileged to do this work.

To everyone across the world who has followed my journey—from the MySpace days to Instagram, from my podcast *The House Medium* to my Patreon—your support and encouragement fuel me every single day. You inspired me to write this book. I asked you to push me, and push you did. Every reminder, every nudge helped more than you know.

To my siblings — Aubyn, Tanya, Laurie, and Jared — thank you for teaching me lessons you didn't even know you were teaching.

To my friends who embraced my weirdness, accepted me as I am, and always encouraged me to stay true to myself — thank you for loving me in the realest way.

To my son's father — thank you for giving me the greatest gift: our son. Thank you for being a wonderful father and, yes, for introducing me to a little witchcraft and the witchy ways (you know you did).

To my Aunt Betty — who always told me, "Get writing that book!" Thank you for being my biggest cheerleader. May I live to be 91 and as sharp as you are.

To my mother-in-law — thank you for seeing the magic in this world and accepting me exactly as I am from day one. Another badass witch in my corner.

To my mother, who brought me into this world, loved me, wanted me, and left too soon — I feel you and hear you with me every day. And to the mother who raised me — thank you for teaching me strength, for showing me how to speak up and fight when needed. You left too soon as well, but I carry your strength always.

To my father — thank you for teaching me kindness, patience, and grace. You always reminded me to find the sun, even in the darkest moments.

To my husband — my best friend, my greatest ally. You've healed parts of me I didn't know were broken. You are the smartest, funniest person I've ever met, and I am your biggest fan. If we were stuck in an elevator together, we'd talk and laugh for hours like we just met. You make life feel like an adventure. I love you. FACT! (Dwight.)

To my son — you are the reason I wrote this book. When you came into my life, it was like someone turned the lights all the way up. You've made me want to be a better person and a better reader. Your compassion and your mind will change the world someday, and I can't wait to watch. Thank you for choosing me to be your mother. I must have done something right. I love you always.

I want to thank Little Adela — thank you for allowing me to heal by writing this book. Thank you for keeping me safe all those years. But I've got it from here. We made it. We're still learning and growing, but now we can let go of the pain from the past and allow ourselves to keep expanding.

We have our own family now — one we love, and who loves us back. So go play. Be free. Enjoy this life. I'll see you soon.

www.ingramcontent.com/pod-product-compliance
Lightning Source LLC
Chambersburg PA
CBHW070329010526
44107CB00004B/464